T0381482

Salmon Canneries

BRITISH COLUMBIA NORTH COAST

Gladys Young Blyth

oolichan books   Box 10 • Lantzville • BC • 1991

Book Size: 8.25x9   Inserts: No   Version: 3

 www.trafford.com

North America & international
toll-free: 1 888 232 4444 (USA & Canada)
fax: 812 355 4082

To my husband, Alex

Contents

Foreword

The original intent of this work was to give a brief report showing the locations, with some pertinent facts and a photograph, of each of the Nass River, Prince Rupert, and Skeena River salmon canning plants.

However, it seemed only fair to those not well acquainted with the salmon fishing industry that a brief chronology of early day to present methods of fishing and processing should be included. This proved a monumental task given the overwhelming dynamics of the industry, its wealth of history and significance in the development of the province of British Columbia.

One fish plant, Royal Fisheries in Prince Rupert, has not been included in this history. Although Royal Fish did install a salmon canning line on an experimental basis and did process a pack in 1959 and 1960, the plant was never considered a salmon cannery. Instead, like Atlin Fish and several other smaller plants in Prince Rupert, it has operated as a producer of fresh and frozen fish.

Where the names of plant managers were known they have been included in the manuscript. Many have been left out, not from oversight, but for lack of availability and the extra time essential for more extensive research.

Introduction

Historically, the Tsimpsean and Haida Indian people were the first fishermen to fish the waters on British Columbia's north coast. Their nations thrived and were never hungry when the salmon gathered in the waters off the shores of their villages, where the rivers and the ocean came together. For every year the primordial instincts of maturing salmon drew them from the far reaches of the Pacific Ocean back to the mouths of their home rivers. By then, having attained peak maturity, they were ready to journey upstream to the place of their birth. There the salmon would mate, spawn, and die.

First to arrive in early spring was the chinook (king, quinnt, spring, tyee), largest of all the five species of salmon. It could weigh anywhere up to a hundred pounds (45 kg) or more. Its flesh was rich and succulent, fit for a great feast. The sockeye (red) followed. Abundant, weighing from five to ten pounds (2–5 kg) at maturity, its bright red flesh was of high nutritive value. An interesting characteristic of this species was its body colour change at spawning to a brilliant red, while the head remained green.

Coho (medium, red, silver, coho) spawned later, in the fall. Its weight at maturity was from six to 12 pounds (3–6 kg). The chum salmon (dog salmon, qualla, keta, calico) usually weighed eight to eighteen pounds (4–8 kg). Its flesh was light in colour and made fine smoked fillets. Pink salmon (humpback) was the smallest and the most numerous of all the species. During spawning the males developed a pronounced hump, or significant ridge, on their backs. They weighed three to ten pounds (1–5 kg) at maturity and their flesh was pink.

All five species of the Pacific Salmon have the same life pattern, with variations in stages of maturation and in size. Each, in its own cycle of development, migrates to the ocean several weeks after hatching in its home stream. After two, or more, years, depending on the species, it returns to its birth place to repeat the mating, spawning, dying process.

Every year the Indian fishermen, caught up in the rituals of the First Salmon Ceremony, watched the "jumpers" and checked the momentum of the migration at the mouths of the Nass and Skeena rivers. Their dugout canoes, armed with spears and clubs that had been prepared during the winter months, were ready for the harvest. Dip-nets were ready, too. These were made from dried stems and roots of nettles and formed into a bag. The first salmon caught would be ritually presented by the Shamans to the Chiefs of the tribes. It was a time of thanksgiving to the salmon who had voluntarily sacrificed themselves so the Indian people could live.

Likewise, those tribes indigenous to the upper reaches of the same rivers watched and waited for their share of the harvest. On the Babine Lake-River systems, the headwaters of the Skeena, and along the Nass River, the fishermen used nets, weirs, and traps to catch their fish. Weirs were the most popular. These obstructions in the river permitted the water to flow through, but hampered, or held back, the fish from swimming upstream. With a natural reluctance to retreat downstream, the salmon's instincts drove them on until they bunched up behind the weirs. They were easily

For many centuries the Indian people of the Skeena and Bulkley river valleys have fished the salmon in its migration up the rivers to the spawning grounds. One of the most popular and productive points, known as Morice Canyon, is on the Bulkley River. Here, the Indian fisherman uses spears and dip-nets to catch the fish.
PAC/C6917

taken by the fishermen. These methods were efficient enough to fill acres of drying racks with the split sides of salmon for smoke cure and weather drying.

The Indian method of preservation was adopted by the early European explorers and fur traders coming into British Columbia. The Hudson's Bay post at Fort Simpson in 1835, and later in Hazelton, further introduced the method of preserving fish with salt, something their company had done successfully at Fort Langley on the Fraser River. Salmon, cleaned and trimmed, were split in two lengthwise and salted down in large barrels called tierces. Full, they weighed from five hundred to eight hundred pounds. This venture proved commercially viable for both local and export markets and was the forerunner of several independent salteries on the coast.

Eventually entrepreneurs recognized the value of a fishery resource that was available, unrestricted, and seemingly inexhaustible. They also realized that it was essential an improved method of preserving salmon be found. At that time, around 1870, the stumbling experimentations of preserving foods by canning had evolved to some success in the province of New Brunswick, on the Sacramento and Columbia Rivers in the United States, and on the Fraser River in British Columbia.

In time, and with considerable trial and error in this new technology, a number of fish plants that had begun as salteries branched into canning. For a while there were both salteries and canneries, or a combination of the two, along the coast.

All early fish canneries were located on river estuaries or at the mouth of a small stream, usually in a sheltered bay or inlet. Clean, fresh water was essential in the canning process and to supply the needs of the community of workers involved in the industry.

Some canneries were built on pilings over the water, others along the beach. Each consisted of a cleaning house (gut shed), filling room, soldering department, cooking bathroom, and storage warehouse. There was also a net and boat service building, boiler house, blacksmith shop, and machine shop. Many plants maintained a can-making plant, box factory, cannery office, store, post office, and messhouse. Housing for employees consisted of rows of small one- or two-room shacks for Indian workers and separate bunkhouses for employees of Chinese, Japanese, or European extraction. A little more prestigious were the dwellings of the cannery manager and his staff. The original cannery village was a bare-board clump of buildings laced together with rough boardwalks, weathering out the years in isolation—dormant most of the year, but intensely active during the summer months.

At first all salmon processing in the cannery was done by hand with crudely improvised equipment. Cans were laboriously fashioned by hand. They were then filled by hand-fillers with fish that were hand butchered, washed, and cut to size. The lids of the cans were soldered on by hand and each can was hand-tested after cooking. Wooden boxes for shipping the product were constructed of box wood produced by the cannery's own sawmill, or one nearby.

To support the productivity of the cannery, each plant had to maintain a fleet of fishboats and provide gillnets for their fishermen. Usually this was done on a rental basis. However, the more independent troller, and later the seine fishermen, quickly became an integral part of the industry.

Changes brought a gradual mechanization of the industry in the processing methods and in the fishing fleet. Consolidation, high speed technological innovations, and quality controls eventually brought to the industry the degree of sophistication essential to maintain a reputation for consistently high standards of productivity.

A double string of gillnet sailboats in a tow behind a tug which has just left
Balmoral Cannery in the background. Each of the double-enders is rigged with a
sail, a pair of oars, and a salmon gillnet and manned with a crew of two men. Note
the pup tents that have been erected on some of the boats, probably because of a
cold wind, for the photo shows there is still snow on the mountains. A patrol vessel,
probably a fisheries boat, travels alongside the tow.   PAC/PA 40961

8

From the beginning of salmon fishing the industry supplied most of their gillnet fishermen with rental boats and nets. In time this changed, so that many fishermen owned their own fishboats and gear.

The first boats were flat-bottomed and powered by sail and the use of ten-foot wooden oars. These small craft were good only on the inside waters, sheltered from the open seas.

Columbia River and Collingwood round-bottom double-enders replaced them. These were larger vessels built for a crew of two men. They were eighteen to twenty-six feet in length, approximately seven feet wide and designed with a sharp-cut stern and bow. The hulls were of lapstreak construction. Like the skiffs, they were powered by sail and a strong man at the oars, but because of size and manoeuvrability they gave fishermen greater latitudes in less protected waters.

On board there was space for a pup tent, or an improvised sail shelter on the fo'c'sle, which provided a little more comfort than a rocky beach at night. A primus, or Swede stove (or one fashioned from a cut-down five gallon coal oil can) served for cooking and a little warmth. The remainder of the vessel was assigned to fish catches, net storage, a lantern float (used for marking the far end of a gillnet in a night set), and a handmade roller on the stern which aided in the setting and hauling of the net. Later, the pup tent gave way to what was known as the doghouse—a low planked in area on the bow which provided crawl space for shelter. A rock, tied to a piece of old line, served as an anchor. These new style double-ender boats came to the north coast in 1897.

Because of their greater adaptability to outside waters, the double-enders were towed by powerful steam or gasoline tugs to the fishing grounds beyond the river mouths. In the towing they were attached by beckets to the long tow-line, single file, behind the tug. Sometimes the tugs had two tow-lines in operation—a double string of fishboats.

A becket was a small piece of rope spliced into the main tow-line approximately every thirty to forty feet. Through the beckets gillnet vessels tied into the tow-line, fore and aft, one astern of the other. The late Bill Lawson, a fisherman, remembered fastening a rope from the cleat of his double-ender around the tow rope of the tug. To let go, the fisherman first released the bow. When the current swung the boat free, he released the stern line. It was a tricky process and fishermen became adept at it if they did not wish to run afoul of another fishboat. In this manner hundreds of fishboats representing several canneries would, at a selected area, release their beckets and quickly clear the path of the boats behind them.

The two men who manned each boat were a fisherman and a boat-puller, oftentimes a young boy, who rowed the vessel. Their linen gillnets were rectangular in length and width with a diamond-shaped mesh, forty-five to sixty meshes deep, depending on the species of salmon to be fished. Length was around two hundred fathoms. They were heavy, cumbered with cedar-wood floats spaced along

Gillnetting

one side to hold the net on the surface, and a series of lead weights similarly spaced along the opposite side to hold the mesh down, suspended curtain fashion, from the surface. Both the rowing and the fishing were jobs for men with strong backs.

The start of a fishing week was usually Sunday evening, when a signal was given by cannon shot or an explosive discharged at one of the nearby canning plants. This was necessary in order to regulate the industry and because fishermen seldom carried timepieces. Upon the signal, usually six o'clock, the boat-pullers would begin rowing, each in a chosen direction, while their companion fishermen cast the nets over the side or stern of the fishboats. Truly the weekly openings got off to a thundering ovation with the explosion of the cannon and the sound of thousands of wooden corks and lead weights rumbling over the sides of wooden hulls.

A buoy or flag was used to mark the end of the net during daylight hours. At night, sets were marked by a lighted lantern mounted on a wooden float adrift at the end of the net.

In the same manner as a fisherman set his net, he pulled it in, hand-over-hand, while the boat-puller rowed toward it. On some occasions they worked along the length of the net, lifting sections and removing fish. The salmon, caught by their gill-covers in the mesh, were picked out and tossed into bins or onto the floor of the fishboat. Once the net was stripped of fish it was re-set. At the end of a fishing day (or night) the fishboats were towed to a nearby scow, or fish camp, and the catches tallied as the fish were peughed aboard the scow. In later years large collecting vessels tended the fishing fleet, picking up the catches directly from the boats and taking them back to the canneries.

For easy recognition by their company tenders, fishboats were painted a designated colour representative of the fishing company and cannery for which they fished. Eventually, distinguishable flags, in solid or combination colours, were flown from the masts or rigging of the fishboats.

Fishing outside the river mouths, having begun in the middle of June, usually lasted to ten weeks. Each weekend a twenty-four hour closure was imposed, signalled by the firing of the cannon on Friday or Saturday. This regulation allowed a calculated escapement of salmon up the rivers for the purpose of spawning. The regulations changed through the years, as the industry grew, to provide for adequate escapement.

During closure times fishermen were towed back to the cannery. Often they elected to drag their fishnets in the tow to clean them, which slowed down the speed of the tug. At the cannery, nets were hauled ashore and washed in wooden tanks, which contained a tanning brine of bluestone and salt dissolved in boiling water. This treatment was to remove fish slime, bacteria, and other deleterious matter and generally help to preserve the net.

Fishermen and boat-pullers, free for a while of confined working and living conditions, enjoyed a respite from hours of rowing and tending nets. A good meal, a bath and clean clothes if there were facilities for such, a chance to nurse their wind and salt-water chapped hands, and a night's rest on something more comfortable than the bare boards of a tossing, unheated ship, boosted their morale. Revitalized, they again joined the tow back to the fishing grounds.

The fishing grounds of the Skeena District extended from a point on the river some twelve miles above the village of Port Essington to Chatham Sound. The fishing in the Sound was largely confined to the waters south of Rachael Island, but in some seasons it was extended out toward Brown Passage, through which the sockeye appeared to enter from the open sea, though a portion of the run was known to come in through Edye Passage to the north of Porcher Island. The first catches were usually made in the vicinity of Rachael Island. But as the season progressed the water was covered with boats, from Port Essington to the Sound.[1]

A canneryman at Nass Harbour Cannery on the Nass River is setting off an explosive to herald the opening of the salmon fishing in the area. Throughout the season this was a weekly duty to signal both the opening and closing. One can imagine the tense silence on the fishing grounds as fishermen, gear ready, waited for the signal. BCARS 51446

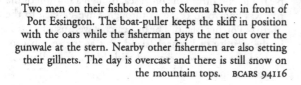

Two men on their fishboat on the Skeena River in front of Port Essington. The boat-puller keeps the skiff in position with the oars while the fisherman pays the net out over the gunwale at the stern. Nearby other fishermen are also setting their gillnets. The day is overcast and there is still snow on the mountain tops. BCARS 94116

12

Fishermen, through experience or by chance, located the most promising fishing spots. The Glory Hole was such a place. Located between a sandbar and the shoreline of Kennedy Island, adjacent to Smith Island, the Glory Hole is to fishermen what a mother lode is to a miner. Like a 'pocket' the Hole is a depression in the tidal flow between the islands where migrating salmon are detained, for a time, at certain stages of the tide. Here, the most successful fishermen were the ones who pushed, shoved, or bullied their vessels and gear into position and held it while the others milled around them. Boats, nets, oars, fish, and men with iron fists and forceful language became embroiled in an annual melee that rewarded them with a boat load of fish, torn and tangled nets, broken oars and masts, and shattered friendships. In this photo, taken at the Glory Hole in 1920, boats show colours and numbers representative of several canneries. Also, a few have progressed to where a small cabin, or doghouse as it was called, has been built on the fo'c'sle.
BCARS 31216

13

Net stowed aboard and sail up, these two fishermen are off Smith or Kennedy Islands, either on their way to the home cannery or looking for a more lucrative fishing area. The boat probably had several owners, for there is a large block patch with an inscription on the centre gunwale and a variety of faded numbers and letters on the stern showing through the weathered paint.
PAC/PA 40977

Before World War Two, changes in the fishing industry took place slowly. In this photo a sailboat is being unloaded onto a scow at the cannery dock while a modern gas boat, with a wheelhouse and cabin, stands by. During the transition only the successful fishermen (or those with enough money) were able to rent or own a gas boat. BCARS 75505

14

A fleet of double-ender gillnet vessels with comfortable wheelhouses and cabins replaced the open sailboats. The photo, taken from Haysport Cannery on the Skeena River, shows Alexandria and Balmoral canneries, left centre, and the town of Port Essington in the distance on the right. The Union Steamship vessel, *Cardena*, is tied up alongside the fishing vessels.   BCARS 88184

At the end of the salmon fishing season, gillnets were taken
from the fishboats, washed in a bluestone (copper sulphate)
solution, mended, and stored for the following year. At the
Mill Bay Cannery on the Nass River in 1913, boats line up
along the dock where each fisherman pulls his net up and
puts it into one of the wooden bluestone tanks to be
washed in the solution.   SPECIAL COLLECTIONS, UBC

16

These large, round, wood-stave tanks were used as containers of bluestone solution in which the cotton and linen gillnets were washed and treated. The solution cleaned the nets of fish slime and algae and helped in the preservation of the netting. Like the fishboats, net racks, scows, and pilings, bluestone tanks were a distinctive part of the cannery setting. They were no longer needed when nylon gillnet web replaced the linen and cotton. BCARS 68296

H 81. B.C Cannerie Disinfecting tanks. F.D.J.

17

H 83. B.C. Canneries. Salmon Nets. J.D.Y.

Cotton, linen, and the modern nylon salmon nets are hung on racks on the net floats where they are mended and hung (attached to) with leadlines and corklines. Between seasons, nets were stored in a large building, usually a net loft above the cannery. During that time, net menders and hangers cared for the nets, getting them ready for the coming season. BCARS 68297

Fishermen mending their gillnets, Skeena River, 1930. In the centre of the photo is the cannery powerhouse with the two chimneys. Note the water barrels atop the roof of the cannery building. They were part of the fire protection most plants had in those days. Notice also the fire bell beside the first barrel. PAC/PA 40981

Modern gillnets made of nylon do not need treating or cleaning. Other than tearing or snagging during fishing, they are more durable and last many more seasons than the two to four years of the linen gillnets. The gillnet boats in the photo are a modification of the double-ender, retaining the cabin and wheelhouse, but with a square stern. Each vessel is equipped with a gillnet drum (roller) on which the net is wound, and a smaller roller on the stern to facilitate setting and hauling the net. Photo taken at Cassiar Cannery on Inverness Passage with Sunnyside Cannery in the distance. AUTHOR

19

As the migrant salmon moved into the river estuaries the fishermen followed as far as the boundaries permitted. Although weather conditions were not as difficult as in outside waters, fishing in the river estuaries was regulated by tides and other trying factors. The fishermen had to row against the strong river currents and work the tides, often at night so the fish could not see the nets.

Gear was put out crosswise on a portion of the river and then angled downstream, curtaining off the path of the salmon. This was usually done before high water slack, that portion of time the tide remained static before ebbing.

About an hour later the net would be picked up and the fish taken on board. In the interim, boats and nets drifted in the wash of the tide while the men drank coffee and endeavoured to find comfort in the heat of their oil-can stoves. However, such respite was often forfeited when nets tangled onto sandbars, drift logs, or debris. And because of the confined fishing area, or the phenomenon of rip tides (a collision of two tides that creates considerable water turbulence), gear sometimes tangled together.

Aside from this, nets were occasionally cut up, or the fishboats were run down, by unsuspecting or unscrupulous larger vessels.

Once salmon fishing ended, around the end of August (or mid-September when coho fishing became part of the industry), the gillnet boats were scrubbed clean, repaired, painted, and stored at the cannery for the winter.

The linen gillnets (and some cotton nets) never lasted more than two to three years at the most. To help preserve them, they were thoroughly washed and tanned to give longer service. But, before this process, they were stripped of cork and lead lines and boiled in water for at least an hour.

One of the formulas for preserving nets was recorded in Catalogue No. 9, Edward Lipsett Limited:

The following formula has been found to give good results, and to materially assist in obtaining longer water service from nets. For tanning use 25 to 30 pounds of cutch for each 100 pounds of netting. Dissolve half this quantity in water. Use boiling water so that you can get the cutch to dissolve quickly. Stir well. When completely dissolved, add sufficient cold water to bring the quantity of liquid up to 50 gallons.

Put your net in and raise the temperature to a few degrees below the boiling point. Keep the netting under the liquid and allow it to cool slowly. Allow same to remain there for 48 hours, then take the net out and dry it. After this is done add the other half of the cutch to the old liquid and repeat the operation.

Do not let fire strike against the boiler in which you have the net or liquid. The boiler containing your net should be placed inside another receptacle filled with water on the bottom sides, and this water should be heated directly by the fire under same, and in this way your cutch will be brought to a boiling point without any risk. Fire direct to the boiler containing the net and liquid is very dangerous to the netting.

Follow this treatment with sodium bi-chromate, and for each 100 pounds of netting use 2 or 3 pounds of chrome. Mix this well in a tub of water, and after it is properly dissolved add sufficient cold water to bring the quantity up to 50 gallons. See that it is well mixed before putting the net into same. With this quantity of sodium bi-chromate you can leave the netting in the liquid for three hours, but no longer.

During this period the netting should be thoroughly washed in cold water and then allowed to dry. To enable the drying to be carried out properly, hang the netting in such a way that a good current of air will be passing through it. Do not put it on a stone or sand in the sun. At the end of the fishing season, if nets are to be tanned, it should be done before putting them in storage.[2]

Another method of preservation was done by washing the netting in raw linseed oil, then wringing it out on a sturdy wringer before air-drying in a shed for three weeks. The linseed oil gave it a yellowish cast. Thereafter, treatments in the bluestone (copper sulphate) solution gave the netting a green tinge.[3]

After World War Two, linen nets were replaced by the more durable nylon mesh, which did not require treatment and lasted for many years of fishing.

Similarly, changes in gillnet fishboats were minimal compared to the postwar years. The original double-ender continued to retain its basic features—the V-bottom, wide beam, solid construction, with slightly raised bow and duck-like characteristics.

Aside from changes in size and the incorporation of a round or square stern, most innovations were toward power, convenience, and comfort. The first and most notable was the installation of internal combustion engines for propulsion.

Although fishermen on the Fraser River were permitted for many years to use boats driven by gas engines, this was not allowed on the north coast until 1924. One theory holds that the ban was imposed by the Provincial Government in Victoria, B.C. through an Order-In-Council.[4]

Another hypothesis surmises that the prohibition was a decision of north coast fishing companies who owned most of the fishing vessels. They did not wish to invest money toward powering their fishboats.[5] Theoretically, the ban was lifted in 1924 to relieve the congestion of motorized vessels on the Fraser River.

To accommodate an engine, the sailboat's centreboard was removed and a shaft-log built in. A propeller was added and the large rudder was replaced by a smaller one. A metal basket-like cover called a net guard was installed over the propellor to protect it from other drifting nets and debris.

The first engines, on the Fraser River in 1910 and on the Skeena in 1924, were no more than three to five horsepower and could attain a speed of a good strong tide. But they were a convenience that replaced the task of rowing, except when the engine broke down. Eventually they were useful in the control of such amenities as a winding drum, a large spool-like roller that could be activated to haul in a gillnet—liberating the fishermen from a punishing task.

Comfort in the ship's design evolved just as slowly as did power and conveniences. Cabin housing replaced the pup-tent or doghouse in the early years up to the late 1920s, and later on, a trunk cabin—a sort of crawl space for built-in bunks and a small galley with a wood and coal burning cast iron stove—was added. Eventually the standard postwar gillnet boat was built to lengths of twenty-six to forty feet, depending on the means and whims of the owner. Naturally, the incorporation of power, conveniences, and comfort into boat design also depended on the means and whims of the owner.

For power, gas combustion engines were supplanted by higher speed diesel units. Engine weight and bulk were cut down, and more power was added to give even more speed, travel range, and power controls in the use of gear.

The first navigational convenience was a compass. This replaced the old sight and sound system when fishermen sailed by familiar landmarks or gauged their whereabouts by bouncing sound off the craggy shoreline. Eventually fishermen learned to read and use nautical charts of the coast. Prior to the Second World War, the echo sounder was invented. This instrument recorded on paper the underwater terrain over which the ship travelled, as well as any schools of fish in the area. And while the echo sounder provided an underwater relief of the ocean floor, another invention, radar, mapped a clear outline of the surface area, showing up the shoreline, drift-logs and seagulls.

After 1936 the radio-telephone became available to fishboats and packers. This instrument gave direct communication between home plants and members of the fishing fleet, to provide better shore control of the industry. The radio-telephone quickly became a comfort against loneliness, isolation, and distress—a life-line in an emergency and a means of visiting a neighbour fisherman or someone at home.

Another amenity that added comfort to the fisherman's lot was the larger wheelhouse. This provided space for housing navigational equipment, a compact galley equipped with a propane or oil-burning stove, and comfortable sleeping quarters. Built-in holding tanks with pumping systems for supplies of water and fuel also became standard equipment.

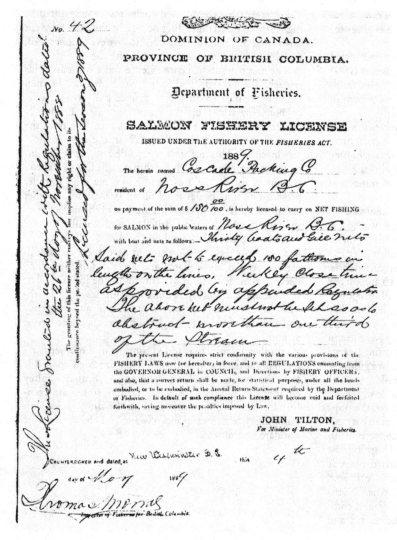

This is a salmon fishery license issued to the Cascade Packing Company on the Nass River in 1889. The license is for thirty boats and gillnets issued in accordance with regulations dated November 26, 1888 by the Department of Fisheries under the authority of the *Fisheries Act* in the Dominion of Canada.

22

Troll Fishing

Early in the development of the fishing industry, before 1900, there emerged the hand-troller, or row-boater, sometimes referred to as skiff fishermen. Transient, and maverick at heart, like the native Indian who used the same methods before them, they lived in rough board shacks on the beaches and fished the daylight hours. They began with anything from dugout canoes to skiffs and eventually used double-enders, which were forerunners of the modern troller.

Each morning at dawn they launched their skiffs down a runway on the beach and at night hauled them in again above the high tide mark. The interim hours, day-in and day-out, weather permitting, were spent fishing around the kelp beds for the coho salmon. They fished five months of the year and longer if they worked the chinook salmon runs in early spring.

The rowboat men propelled their vessels with sails, or manually by using oars, and fished a single line of gear. One end of the line was slip-knotted around the thigh of their leg. The other was equipped with a hand-made spinner (cut and hammered out of spoon metal), a hook, swivel, split rings, some piano wire and a half or one-pound lead weight, depending on the depth to be fished. Until mid-July, when herring became mature enough for bait, spinners were used almost exclusively to attract the fish to the hook. Sometimes a strip of skin and flesh was cut from the gill-openings of a freshly caught salmon and used as bait. When the herring were ready, the fishermen used a rake to fish them aboard.

The herring rake was attached to a ten to fourteen-foot handle. Its leading edge was fitted with teeth made from a strand of stiff wire cable cut in even lengths and spaced approximately one-half inch apart. The rake was cradled in the crook of a forked stick cocked up over the bow of the skiff. On seeing the herring the fishermen would swing it out and down, reversing the teeth among the fish, then bring it up, hand-over-hand. The impaled herring would then be shaken onto the boat to be used as bait.

Hand trolling gave way to the use of poles—first a single rod, then branching into two, port and starboard. Cut from the forest, these first poles were aptly called "poverty sticks." They were about the length of the boat and were mounted on hinges on either side of the mast. While fishing, the poles were lowered over the water at an angle to the boat, about 45 degrees. In time two more poles were mounted on the bow of the boat and all four poles could be swung out to a position where the lines and gear would not tangle together.

The troll lines were attached to the top of each pole, one end running down the pole to the deck of the boat, the other out into the ocean. Lines were made up of several components. A length of cotton line, interspersed with lead weights, was fastened next to the top of the pole. Another length of line known as imported Irish linen cuttyhunk, olive green in colour and having anywhere from 18 to 144 pound test, was joined to the cotton line. Leader lines were attached to the main line at regular intervals. These were of cuttyhunk. A short piece of piano wire joined them to

23

Trolling

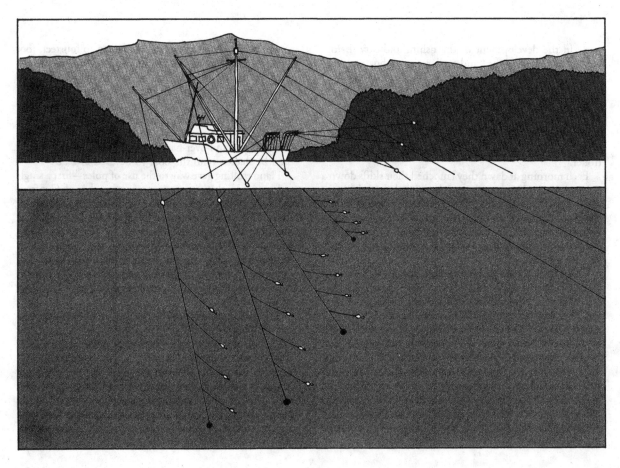

A fleet of trolling boats tied up at a dock in Prince Rupert, 1950s. The main trolling poles were mounted on hinges alongside the mast. When fishing, they were rigged with gear and lowered over the water at an angle to the boat. Two more poles were mounted on the bow. These, too, were rigged with gear and lowered over the water at an angle. The bow-poles, when not in use, were lowered toward the wheelhouse to rest on a cross-arm of the mast. Later, fishermen rigged their fishboats for a combination of fishing methods: troller-gillnetter, etc.   ROSS

hooked steel flashers. All was put together with swivels, rings, and bobbers (made from rubber tubing to take up the tension on the lines). Later, at the top of the pole a bell was attached to herald a "strike."

A troll fishermen's only other equipment was a hand-made dip-net, a gaff wired onto a wooden handle, a tarp or ground sheet, a grub box, a five gallon water can, a cut-down coal oil can for a stove, a blanket, and if he could afford them, a slicker and a pair of gumboots. Food was purchased from the fish collecting boats that made a daily circuit of the trollers.

Although troll methods did not change with the years, eventually the trolling boats, their source of power, and their gear did change.

Skiffs graduated to carvel planked double-enders, then became larger, with housing and built-in accommodations. Gas engines replaced the sails and oars. And high-speed diesel engines replaced the gasoline engines. Gear became more sophisticated, with a selection of factory-made blocks, pulleys, spacers, bells for alerting a strike, pole springs, cannon-ball sinkers, connectors, wobblers, plugs, spoons, and spinners. Multi-strand stainless steel line, with a minimum breaking strain of 630 pounds, replaced cotton and linen lines.

Further, the back-breaking task of setting and hauling gear by hand changed with the invention of the gurdy, which was used to wind the individual troll lines out and in. They were first controlled manually by a positive friction clutch, then mechanically, with the advent of the gasoline engine.

Greater engine power, improvements in gear and ac-commodation, and the acquisition of such navigational aids as the radio telephone, radar, and the depth sounder, gave the troller an unlimited range. Refrigerated holding capacities for their fish catches eliminated the dangers of fish spoilage.

While most of the trolling is done in one day trips some of the larger boats have hold capacity to enable them to go on two to three week trips.

They carry ice and ice each day's catch in the hold. These trips are usually brought right to the cannery. In this way the troller receives a little more for his fish as he has saved the cannery the packing charge.[6]

Like the gillnetter, the troller evolved slowly. It took many years to move forward from a skiff with a single line of hand-operated gear to a large diesel-powered vessel that could handle eight lines and forty spoons at once. This capacity, of course, is strictly governed by changing regulations that may permit eight, six, or even four lines.

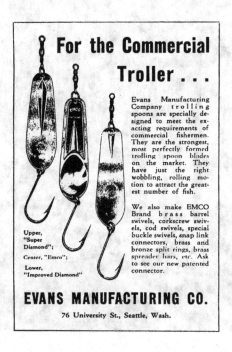

Seine Fishing

As the gillnetter and troller had done before them, the seine fishermen began under stringent conditions—open boats, no mechanical power, and the most rudimentary gear. And, like the gillnetter and troller, their basic method of fishery has not changed throughout the years.

The first seine fishermen worked with large rowboats, each thirty to forty feet in length. A crew of men propelled them with the use of oars. They worked in tandem with a large scow, which was equipped with a hand winch for the pursing up of the heavy, cumbersome nets.

The era of power seine boats began early in the century. They were open boats with a small house to cover the engine, but no provision for living accommodations. A well-deck aft covered the propellor shaft and supported a hand-operated winch. Fish catches were also stored there. The net was kept on a platform on the stern of the vessel. It was no longer necessary to work in tandem with a scow. The skiff was then used to anchor one end of the net while the seiner made the circle around a school of fish and returned to it. The net with its catch of fish was then pursed up to a position where the salmon could be loaded directly aboard the seine boat.

Eventually these seiners were fitted with a deck, mast, forecastle for the crew, a pilot-house, cargo boom, a platform aft called a "table" for decking the seine net, and a mechanically driven winch.

... the vessels engaged in purse-seining are power craft from 60 to 80 feet in length, broad-beamed and square-sterned, fitted with a platform aft which, mounted on a pivot, can be turned in any direction. Upon this turntable, the seine net is piled ready to set.

The vessel cruises about, and when the school of fish has been sighted, she heads toward it. If the skipper judges the school is worthwhile making a set for, he orders the skiff or rowboat to be launched. The man in the small boat has taken one end of the seine with him and keeps rowing while the vessel moves to surround the school—the net running out over her stern as she makes the circle.

In due course the larger craft has run the whole of the seine out and joins up with the skiff. The two ends of the net are brought together aboard the seiner and the ends of the purse line are taken to the winch and hauled in by power. This closes the bottom of the net like the drawstrings of a purse, and prevents the fish from escaping through the bottom of the seine—if the fishermen are quick enough.

When the net has been closed at the bottom, the job of hauling-in the seine begins. The mesh is fetched aboard the boat until the fish are enclosed in but a small portion of it. By this time they are in a solid, flipping, milling mass alongside the vessel. A dip-net, sometimes called a bailer or brailer, operated by power and manipulated by one of the crew, is dipped into the mass of fish and swung inboard. When all the catch has been taken into the vessel's hold, the net is restowed ready for setting again.

Seining is a method of fishing that calls for speed—particularly in the setting of the net to surround the school, and the pursing-up to ensure that it doesn't escape. Very frequently the school evades the encircling manoeuvre. At other times, when surrounded by the seine and the crew are in the act of pursing-up, the fish will "dive the twine" as the saying is, and make their escape through the partially-closed bottom and the seine will have accomplished nothing but a 'water-haul' for their trouble. It is one of the most exciting methods of fishing, but if luck holds, and the crew is smart, it yields enormous hauls of fish at times.[7]

In the progression of the seining industry, seine boats became a complicated mass of gear with chain drives, overhead shafting, right-angle drives, Model-T clutches, and automotive rear ends. Hydraulic equipment was introduced, providing changes in overall efficiency. Seine tables

Purse Seining

Seine fishermen setting their nets in Captain's Cove, Pitt Island in 1927. The centre seiner has formed a circle in the water with his net surrounding a body of fish. A second seine boat, in the distance, has launched a rowboat. A man in the rowboat is preparing to take one end of the net and to keep rowing while the larger vessel moves to surround a school of fish.   BCARS 75520

were replaced by hydraulically controlled power blocks for handling the nets, and hydraulically driven drums—a large spool-type roller, larger than a gillnet roller, onto which a seine net could be rolled aboard, or from which it could be dispensed into the sea.

Modern seiners with large capacity holds were equipped with refrigeration or a brine cooling system. Power was supplied by heavy duty diesel engines. The latest in communications systems and technological aids to navigation became standard equipment.

Comfortable living quarters for the skipper and his crew became an essential part of life on the fishing grounds. The seine fishermen then had the option of remaining at sea long enough to fill the hold of the ship with fish, or to take a full share of the government regulated quota.

No change in vessels, equipment, or amenities was more dramatic than in that most essential component of seining—the seine net. The first nets were made of varying lengths of heavy cotton web, usually twelve hundred feet long and seventy feet deep. When set in the water, like a circular curtain, the seine was supported at the top by a series of cork floats threaded on the headline. The bottom of the netting was kept fully submerged by heavy weights or leads attached to a rope connected to the foot of the seine. These top and bottom lines were known as the corkline and the leadline. To the foot of the seine, below the leadline, at regular intervals a series of brass rings were attached through which a stout cable called a purse-line was threaded. This was for the purpose of 'pursing up,' or closing the bottom of the seine net when a school of fish was surrounded.

The net itself was made of several components of mesh. A heavier twine than the corkline and body web was woven into the net along the bottom in support of the leadline. The sturdiest and most durable gauge of web was woven into the bunt end, the part of the net that must contain the bulk of a pursed load of fish.

Another method of using a seine net eventually became illegal:

...The drag seine has no purse line on the bottom and one end of the net is made fast ashore while the other is carried out in a boat to surround a school of fish that may be passing close to the beach. The boat encircles the school and fetches its end of the seine ashore. The whole seine is then dragged onto the beach by horses, tractors or by manpower.[8]

As with the linen gillnetting, before nylon was available, cotton seine netting shipped from the factory in 250 pound bales had to be cutched and chromed. It was then further treated with tar before attaching the leadline and corkline.

Tarring has been found an excellent method of preservation, especially for heavy nets such as seines. It is simple and the expense is not a serious item. Coal tar has been found to give the most satisfactory results. The greatest drawback to coal tar is the increased weight that results, by approximately 75 percent.

To get the best results from this tarring process, nets or twine should not be too dry, otherwise the fibre will absorb too much of the tar, and this has a tendency to stiffen the net when same is in use. Damp the material slightly before carrying the tarring process into effect. Some fishermen claim it is a good thing to put the net out for a few minutes in a good shower of rain.

To help keep the product soft and pliable, add a few pounds of yellow tallow to each 50 gallons of tar. The tar should be brought to a boil and the net allowed to run through the solution slowly. As it comes out of the tub it should be allowed to pass between rubber rollers to enable all the surplus tar adhering to the netting to be removed. This tarring process does not require to be repeated.[9]

The other netting instrument, the brailer, was also made up of seine webbing. Formed like a large dip-net, it was used to remove fish from the seine net. It, too, had a rope or cable threaded through an open bottom edge. When full, with the cable drawn up like a drawstring, the brailer was swung around manually (eventually mechanically) from its station on the scow, and later the seiner, and dumped aboard.

The only change in seine webbing has been from cotton twine to the more resistant nylon. Special treatment with cutch, chrome, and tar is no longer necessary. Bales of netting shipped from the factory can readily be made to specifications, having the leadline and corkline attached at the fish plant.

Canning Season Preliminaries

Early in the spring, prior to the canning season, which usually opened around the middle of June, the plant manager or owner of each canning firm hired the key staff. These men were the foreman, a net boss, Japanese boss fisherman, Indian boss fisherman, and a boss Chinaman. This system prevailed until the late 1940s.

The foreman was hired to supervise or maintain the plant in everything from the building of a cannery to the general maintenance of machinery, equipment, and boat repairs. Aside from resourcefulness and versatility on the job, the foreman required diplomacy and tact in order to handle employees from several ethnic backgrounds.

The net boss's responsibility was the making, treatment, repair, and care of the fishnets. Under his supervision, nets were made from imported twines (in the very early days of the industry); they were hung with leadline and corkline and the torn ones mended throughout the season. The net man employed a crew of men to treat the nets. Their jobs were to tan and colour the netting in preservative of cutch and chrome, or raw linseed oil. During the fishing season they were responsible for the bluestoning (copper sulphate) process of cleaning the nets and at the end of the fishing season for storing them, usually in a cannery loft.

The Japanese and Indian boss fishermen acted as liaison men between management and their respective groups. They were responsible for the hiring of fishermen and then for serving as spokesmen to handle employment problems and misunderstandings arising from language differences.

The boss Chinaman and his crew were hired under a contract system through negotiations with a Chinese contracting firm and the canning company. The contractor made an agreement with a cannery on a price for a season's work based on the estimates for production and then hired accordingly. The Chinese crew then became responsible, under the cannery manager, for processing the salmon pack, from the pre-season manufacturing of cans to unloading fish scows and boats, butchering the salmon, filling cans, cooking, testing, and boxing up the product for shipment.

SEMI OR READY-FORMED CANS

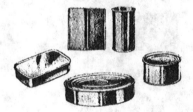

◄ Millions of cans were individually cut to a pattern, assembled, and soldered by hand in the early days. Later on they were punched out on manually controlled machines. This is what a warehouse full of one-half pound cans looked like in 1913.   BCARS 84149

The body of a charcoal burner stove once used by Chinese can-makers at North Pacific Cannery. The photo shows the chimney and lid openings, but the hearth is missing from the front. The little burners, usually about 18 inches tall (although some later models were larger and had manual blowers) were stoked with charcoal made at a charcoal pit. Soldering irons were laid into the hearth and heated, then used to apply solder in the making of the cans. The burners were usually mounted on a tray of sand on the work bench.
AUTHOR

This giant mound of tin clippings—six feet tall and five feet wide—was made up of an accumulation of sixty years of tin scraps dropped through the Inverness Cannery floor onto the beach by Chinese can-makers. Beginning in 1876, the tin cuttings adhered to one another, clinging tenaciously through the daily tide cycles until 1973 (ninety-seven years) when the cannery complex burned down. The mound of tin, a monument to the early can-makers, was destroyed.
AUTHOR 1972

The Re-form Line at Old Oceanside Cannery, Ocean Dock, Prince Rupert. Collapsed cans, shipped 330 to a case in the same boxes that normally cased 48 assembled tall cans, were re-formed, or automatically re-shaped to cylindrical perfection on these machines. They then passed through a flanger and a double seamer, and the bottoms to the cans were attached. WRATHALL

The first task of the Chinese boss and his crew upon arrival at a cannery was the making of cans to contain the salmon product. Materials and supplies for assembling the cans, as well as other plant necessities, had to be unloaded from the freighters that stopped in at all coastal points on their annual spring cannery trip.

Cargo for making cans consisted of heavy bundles of sheet tin imported from England, kegs of solder (an alloy used to join metal parts), and containers of flux (a substance used to help metals fuse together).

Charcoal had to be brought in from the charcoal burning pits somewhere in the vicinity of the canning plant. On the Skeena River these pits were located at Port Essington and Port Edward.

Charcoal was a form of carbon made by partially burning alder wood in an airless kiln. It was used to fuel small cast-iron stoves called charcoal burners or braziers. The stoves were installed in the tinsmith shop over a tray of sand on the work benches.

The charcoal burner heated the soldering iron, the main tool for assembling the cans. The tip of the soldering iron was made to varying shapes and weights, suitable for a specific task. Shaped from brass or copper, it was attached to a metal rod and the other end sheathed in a wooden handle. The worker placed the tip of the iron into the opening of the charcoal burner. Once heated it was used to apply solder to the cut and shaped can bodies. Other instruments were flux brushes, grippers, clinchers, and scrape awls, all essential to the process.

Can bodies were measured and cut to the right size from 12 × 18 inch (approximately) sheets of tin by using large shears. Later on in the development of the industry they were cut on a table which was equipped with a long knife called squaring shears. It had a guide to help keep the pattern uniform.

The body was then rounded on a sheet-iron covered cylinder called a reamer. Overlapping edges were held together by a clinching tool until the sides were soldered together. The worker applied two pieces of solder to the edges, and gave it a rub with the hot soldering iron, thus sealing it airtight.

Tops and bottoms for the cans were drawn in a circle on the tin plate with a compass and then cut by hand with the shears. They were individually crimped by a hand press to fit the can body.[10]

In those days cans were made so that the lid fitted inside of the body and the body had a burr flaring outward so as to facilitate lids being put on.[11]

Some of the first attempts were oval shaped cans. However, these were not successful. The cylinder shaped cans, one-pound talls and later the one-half pound flats, proved more suitable. Eventually one-quarter pound cans also became standard.

By 1890 the lids and bottoms were stamped out by a foot operated die and capper machine, which crimped them on the cylinders preparatory to the soldering. Can production was then on a ratio of 500–700 cases per day which handled the catches of about twenty fishboats.

Can-making by hand continued on the north coast until sometime after 1910. Meantime the factory-produced sanitary can, with the top and bottom crimped and side seam soldered on the outside only, was introduced. Eventually a machine was made that crimped the can bodies in a lock and lap device so that soldering became obsolete.

By 1923 the machinery for the can-making plant at North Pacific Cannery on the Skeena River consisted of two slitters, a bodymaker, flanger, two double seamers, and a foot tester. Resin flux was used for soldering in the bodymaking machine, and the solder pot was heated by coal oil. The North Pacific can manufacturing plant continued to operate until 1936.

For a time, many canneries made part of their requirements on site, having the remainder shipped in from the factories in Vancouver. By 1933 the factories could produce cans at a rate of 250 per minute.

During the 1930s a new factory method of making cans was introduced. It was known as the Collapsed Can. With this new method the can bodies were flattened at the can factory, packed and shipped, 330 to the case, in the same boxes that normally cased 48 assembled tall cans. At the cannery they were re-formed with machinery that automatically reshaped the bodies to cylinder perfection, then passed them through a flanger and a double seamer and attached the bottoms, nonstop, to the filling machine.

The first cans made by hand were not lacquered to protect them from rust. Storage life was short and spoilage resulted. Painting the cans by hand with a type of red paint was tried, and later on a quick-drying brown lacquer was used. Another method was the use of enamel on the ends of the cans, relying on the labels to protect the bodies from rust. In 1901 a machine for lacquering cans was invented. But it was many years before cans were required to be completely lacquered against rust.

The Federation Brand can label was used by the Mill Bay Cannery on the Nass River as early as 1893.

Early Canning Process

From the beginning, the canning season on the Nass and Skeena Rivers opened in mid-June. Then, as now, salmon converged on the estuaries of these rivers in great quantities, and, having ceased to feed in the change from the salt to fresh waters, were at their optimum condition.

Of all the five species, the sockeye was preferred. This was because of its uniform size, firmness of flesh, high oil content, and its pleasing colour as a canned product. After 1900 the other species of salmon became equally important to the industry.

Canning of salmon in the first years was done by hand under primitive conditions. Buildings were crude, sometimes only a shack on the beach.

Inside the fish-house the canning lines, at the outset, were a series of wooden tables, tanks, and benches. Tables were used for butchering, cleaning, draining, filling cans, weighing, and cooling. The tanks were used for washing the fish, cooking the canned product, and then testing the reliability of the process.

Benches served as work areas for the soldering of cans. Interconnecting the lines of tables, tanks, and benches were chutes, trays, pails, and wicker baskets. These facilitated the movement of the product from one area to another.

The system of processing salmon has remained essentially the same throughout its history. The first canneries unloaded salmon at the docks and then put them through some semblance of a canning line to end up as a tinned product. Evolving systems have maintained the original concept, expanding into manually and eventually mechan-

ically controlled machinery. Today's technology employs high speed machines.

One of the greatest threats to the canning industry was the problem of spoilage—how to keep fish fresh until tinned and how to be certain it was sterilized and sealed for safe marketing.

It began at the unloading dock. At one time fish were indiscriminately peughed from the scows and tenders onto slimy, insect-infested and open docks where they might languish in all kinds of weather until processed or dumped.

Unloaders of the era stood knee-deep in the salmon and pitched them up onto the dock, one-by-one, with a one-tined fork on a long handle called a peugh. Tallymen stood by, counting the fish.

To cut labour costs and waste and to preserve quality, unloading elevators were installed. These were made of two parallels of endless chain on wooden supports that rotated from the water's edge to above the top of the wharf.

Placed on a slant, the elevator chains supported wooden bucket-type crosspieces between them, spaced two feet apart, to serve as containers, or buckets, to receive the salmon. Fish were then peughed into the revolving elevator from the scow at the bottom. At the top the fish fell into chutes that took them to a wooden holding bin. In later years suction pumps that automatically pumped the salmon directly to the holding bin from the scow, or from the hold of a ship, eliminated all handling and peughing.

The holding bins, too, were improved from crude wooden containers to refrigerated aluminum or stainless steel tanks.

37

Before modern hydraulic suction pumps came into use, fish were peughed singly onto a chute, from the packer or scow, by an unloading crew. The fish slid down the chute into a tank of water built into the unloading float. The long arm of the unloading elevator, with built-in buckets, was mechanically operated to take the fish from the scow or boat up to the cannery dock. DOPSON

H43. B.C. Canneries Salmon Cutting Machine FDJ

◄ Salmon contained in wooden holding bins, a step ahead of containing them on the cannery floor or open docks. Modern holding bins are constructed of stainless steel or aluminum and refrigerated to keep the product in prime condition. In the early days, men worked at wooden tables butchering the salmon, removing heads, tails, fins, and entrails. In recent years, highly automated machines have replaced the butchers in a faster, more efficient method of processing.   BCARS 92108

One of the first machines invented for cannery use was the cutting machine. Fish were placed crosswise (horizontally) in the machine. A machine operator manually turned the big lever on the side of the cutter, which elevated salmon into the gang knives at the top. Cut to a selected can size, the chunks of fish fell back into the wooden holding bins. This photo was taken in 1913.   BCARS 81163

40

Salmon grouped along a chute in front of the header machine. Each fish will then go on into the Iron Chink (Iron Butcher) beside the header machine. PAC/PA 40985

◀ This photo taken c1890 shows Indian women working at the cleaning (sliming) tables. They stand at low wooden tables cleaning the fish and washing them in the wooden tank filled with water in front of them. Note the water pipe and hose leading from behind the women and into the tank. There were no electric lights then and obviously no other kind of lighting shown in the photo.
PAC/PA 118162

Women workers at the old Oceanside Cannery, Ocean Dock, in Prince Rupert. Modern sliming tanks are made of stainless steel or aluminum and stationed at waist level. Running water is piped directly above the tanks with individual taps over each cleaning unit. A continuous operating conveyor runs between the two rows of workers.
Cleaned fish are placed on the conveyor and sent on into the processing stream. There is overhead lighting, and the women wear clean white uniforms. PRICE

Later, when cans were filled by filling machines, ▶ underweight cans were automatically ejected onto the patching table. They were "patched" with portions of salmon to bring them up to the prescribed weight. A conveyor returned them to the main canning line.
BCARS 74571

Workers, usually women, filled the cans and then placed them on wooden trays which held 24 one-pound tall cans, or 12 if they were the flat half-pound sizes. These workers are surrounded by empty trays waiting to be filled. Beside them are wicker baskets full of empty cans. Chunks of salmon are strewn in front of them on the long wooden tables.   BCARS 745267

Originally the fillers filled the cans with salmon by hand. Wooden containers of cut salmon were brought to the table by the Chinese workers. The supply of shiny new empty cans were placed on an elevated rack in front of the workers. While some workers stood at the job, others found a comfortable wooden box on which to sit.
BCARS 75297

On the first soldering machines, cans were fed onto a chute and into a rounding wheel to bring the cans into alignment. Each can passed under the drip of a flux tank in preparation for soldering on the lids. They travelled at an angle through a cast-iron trough containing molten solder. The solder was kept heated by furnaces of coal or kerosene beneath the trough. The machine was manually controlled to roll the cans through the solder and onto an after chute. The operation was controlled by a revolving chain system and later by pulleys and belts, as in this photo. BCARS 81166

In the fish-house the Chinese butchers and slitters, or Butcher's Gang as they were called, removed the head, tail, fins, and entrails from each fish and dumped the refuse through a hole in the floor onto the beach. Each butcher could clean up to two thousand fish in a ten-hour day.

The most significant technological changes came with this phase of the canning process. The Iron Chink (now known as the Iron Butcher) so called because it replaced the large crews of Chinese butchers at each plant, was invented. It was readily installed in every canning plant as soon as available, probably about 1910 on the north coast, or when the canning companies could afford to buy one.

This new machine automatically adjusted to each size of fish fed into it—slitting, cleaning, removing the head, tail and fins at the rate of one fish per second. Thus one skilled operator and his assistants operating a butchering machine could replace as many as thirty highly skilled hand butchers. The same machine, with some modifications, is still fundamental to modern day processing.

At first the butchered salmon were carried to the washing tanks by hand. Here they were washed under running water from an open trough, scraped and scrubbed clean, and washed again in a second tank. They were then placed on a draining screen to draw off excess water.

This step of the operation changed to the use of long wooden tables along which several workers could stand. The tables were equipped with an overhead system of water pipes and faucets under which fish could be washed in the flow of water.

This, too, in time was modernized to a double row of sliming tanks of perhaps fourteen to twenty units at which each worker washed the fish beneath a jet of continuously running cold water. The fish were then placed on a conveyor built into the centre partition of the rows of sliming tanks, and sent on to the next stage in the process.

The mechanized conveyor system supplanted the use of buckets, wicker baskets, and wooden chutes. Open troughs were replaced by woodstave pipelines and rubber hoses, gravity fed or pumped, which brought water directly from a lake or a holding dam on a freshwater stream.

Once Chinese butchers stood at a butcher's block for long, tedious hours lopping off can-sized chunks of salmon with razor sharp knives.

One of the first machines invented for cannery use was the cutting machine. Two salmon could be placed in it and cut to size by turning a hand lever. This machine, in turn, was replaced by a rotary power-operated unit with circular saws called gang knives. They were mounted on an axle and spaced to cut salmon to the regulated size.

Later, in modern plants, the cutting machine became a composite part of the continuous processing line.

In the early days, cut salmon were kept on open tables or in bins until the fillers could put them in tins. Or the pieces were sent down a chute into a bucket and carried by workers to the filling tables.

Workers, usually women, filled the cans by hand. They were then placed on trays which held twenty-four of the one-pound, tall cans, or twelve if they were the flat, half-pound size. A good filler could fill twelve trays in four minutes. The trays were then carried to the weighers to be checked for proper weight. At some plants children washed or rubbed the cans clean with a piece of netting.

By 1912 a filling machine had been invented. Each can was filled automatically with fish by means of a plunger at the rate of 75 to 120 per minute. Attached to the filler was an automatic salter which could be regulated to inject a prescribed amount of salt into each can as it went through the machine. Filling machines could be regulated for all sizes of cans. They soon became highly automated, high-speed and complex units of equipment requiring specifically trained operators and technicians to operate.

Even so, for a time, hand-packing continued for flat or odd-sized cans, and for custom packing of sockeye to supply a discriminating English market.

Before weighing machines were invented, women workers weighed each can on a scale. Underweight cans were taken to a table and "patched" with portions of salmon to bring them up to the prescribed weight.

Once weighing machines became an integral part of the canning line the underweight cans were automatically ejected onto the patching table, where adjustments were made by workers. Repaired cans were replaced on the conveyor in the centre of the table and returned to the mainstream.

Initially, filled cans were carried in wicker baskets to the soldering department, where the lids were to be soldered on by hand.

Each lid, crimped to fit over the opening of a can (in some earlier experiments the lids were fitted inside the can), had a hole punched in the centre. This was to allow steam and air to escape in the first cooking.

Before the lid was placed on the can a small piece of waste tin was centred on top of the fish, beneath the hole in the lid. During the cooking process it acted as an escape valve for steam and prevented solder and water from seeping into the product.[12] The lids were then individually soldered on each can by hand.

Later, a soldering machine was used. The full cans, fitted with the lids, were placed one after the other onto a chute and fed to a manually controlled machine. Built over the chute was a tank containing flux, which was adjusted to drip onto the rim of each passing can in preparation for the soldering. At the end of the chute and next to the machine was a rounding wheel, which shaped the cans into uniform alignment under pressure from a lever.

From there they proceeded at an angle, with the lid down, through a narrow cast-iron trough containing molten solder. The machine was under-girded with brickwork, which housed small furnaces fired by coal or kerosene to keep the solder melted. Above the framework and at each end were large pulleys through which a chain system was wound by hand. The chain acted as a control to roll the cans through the solder and onto an after chute.

Once cans were made by machine, or manufactured at a can factory, soldering on lids was no longer necessary.

Instead, a clincher was designed; a machine that fit lids loosely to the can bodies to allow air to escape and yet protect the product from direct contact with the steam heat.

Originally the canned salmon was put through two cooking procedures. The first was to exhaust the air from the can before sealing the vent hole in the lid. The second completed the cooking in a steam box and eventually a retort. In time the two cookings changed to a single retort cooking when the fully automated clincher and vacuum machines became standard cannery line equipment.

At first the sealed cans were placed on racks and lowered into the tester, or exhaust vat, containing boiling water. The water was heated by steam from coal-fired boilers cooking the salmon for seventy-five minutes. The procedure would exhaust the cans of air. The product was then removed and the hole in the lids soldered shut.

This method was replaced by a steam exhaust box. The exhauster was about thirty feet long, having inside it endless diamond chain belts running side by side, which trucked stacked trays of canned salmon, with their lids on, back and forth through steam until they reached the far end.

The method drove off air and insured a sufficient vacuum in the can so that, after cooling, the ends of the cans would remain concave under all conditions and temperatures.

Following this process, the cans were conveyed to the double seamer, which fastened the covers on tightly with a double seam, or crimp. Eventually the steam exhaust box was discarded for the vacuum closing machine. This machine automatically placed the lids on the cans, exhausted the air to create a vacuum, and hermetically sealed on the tops. The new unit became a modern feature built into the canning line.

The second cooking was done then, as now, in large retorts or steam ovens. Original retorts were made of wood but soon changed to the cylindrically shaped metal chambers now in use. Racks of canned salmon were wheeled into the retorts and a heavy door closed, or lowered, before steam was turned on to a pressure of 240 degrees Fahrenheit for about sixty-five minutes. After the double cooking method ended at the turn of the century, the single cooking took a total of approximately ninety minutes, depending on can size, species of salmon, and condition of the fish. Each retort is capable of holding several loaders filled with trays of salmon.

In the early days of canning, the product was tested with wooden mallets to determine if the cans were properly sealed. The mallets were used to tap each can on the lid with a sharp rap. A clear signal indicated a proper seal. A dull sound revealed which cans had not sealed. On the reverse side of the mallet was a sharp instrument which was used to pierce a second hole in the lids of the questionable cans.

Often steam and juice would spurt from the puncture onto the rough board or sawdust floors. Once the pressure subsided, the test hole was brushed clean, a few drops of flux was applied and the hole bonded with solder. These cans were sent back into the cooking later to replace the ones taken from the following batch for repair. By 1913 the reliability of the Sanitary Can replaced the highly skilled bathroom crew (those involved in the cooking and testing process).

After the cooking process was completed, the salmon was wheeled to workmen called washers. They cleaned the cans in a caustic soda bath, rubbing them to remove the grease. Rinsed again by hand, they were trucked to a storage area to cool.

Once more the cans were sounded for leaks, this time by using small steel rods. Leaky cans were removed, perhaps again to be reprocessed. The remainder were left to cool thoroughly before boxing for shipment. In later years the product was cooled immediately after cooking by submersion in a cold water bath and then sent on for inspection and boxing up.

During the early days of no inspections or regulatory controls, it was in the industry's best interest to voluntarily maintain their own quality controls.

Cold storage facilities, introduced on the north coast in 1910, helped to maintain better control over the quality of salmon before canning. Overflows of fish caught in excess of a day's canning capacity were no longer a spoilage risk. They could be kept under refrigeration for another day. It was at this point, too, that the canning industry moved more conclusively into the canning of other species besides the sockeye.

Mandatory controls did come eventually, in 1932, with the Canadian government's system of compulsory inspection under the Meat and Canned Food Act.

As controls, voluntary or imposed, became entrenched in the industry, there was a move toward the utilization of the many tons of fish wastes indiscriminately dumped from the docks. Reduction plants were built in conjunction with some of the canneries. These produced fishmeal and oil from the fish offal, a by-product that proved economically viable.

Another by-product, relevant to the early days, was the making of wooden boxes to contain forty-eight one-pound tall cans or ninety-six half-pound flats, a case amount that became standard in 1876. The boxwood for the containers was obtained from a local sawmill, such as Georgetown, or cannery-owned sawmills at Claxton and Port Essington. Thousands of wooden boxes were made on site.

The boxes were filled by hand with canned salmon, and loaded aboard a coastal steamer for shipment to warehouses in Vancouver and Victoria. The product now is boxed automatically, by machine, in cardboard containers.

Throughout the history of salmon canning from 1870 to 1950, the Chinese contract system was the network of manpower that welded the industry together. From the first crude wooden equipment and open trough system—making boxes and cans by hand—until technology and automation replaced them, the Chinese were the major workforce.

In turn, they hired, and worked alongside, people of many other races, particularly the Indian people who came from the Nass and Skeena rivers to take part in an industry that grew out of the natural resources of their own frontier.

46

Eventually a machine was invented to put the lids on the cans. With progressive modifications this machine automatically placed the lids on the cans, exhausted the air to create a vacuum in the can, and hermetically sealed on the tops.   BCARS 75289

To accommodate the pressure of the soldering machine and to provide an escape for steam in the first hot water test, or first cooking, each can lid had a hole punched in the centre. The sealed cans were placed on racks and lowered into the tester, or exhaust vat, containing boiling water heated by coal-fired boilers. After this initial cooking the product was removed and the centre hole soldered over.   BCARS 81167

Workers using a hot soldering iron, a pail of flux, and a stick of solder deftly close the centre hole in the cans. Beyond them other workers are lowering trays of canned salmon into the exhaust vats.   BCARS 82095

The second cooking of the canned salmon was done in a large, cylindrical, asbestos-covered oven called a retort, for approximately one hour—more or less depending on the size of the cans and the species being processed—at 240 degrees Fahrenheit. The trays were taken in and discharged from the far end of the retort where the photo shows the pulleys for opening and closing the doors. Note the gauges on the retorts for setting the time of entry and discharge. The workman in the centre is washing the cans.   BCARS 84142

When the canned salmon had cooled, usually overnight in a warehouse, each can was tested with a wooden mallet used to hit it on the lid with a sharp rap. A clear signal indicated a proper seal. A dull sound revealed those that had not sealed. On the reverse side of the mallet was a sharp instrument which was used to pierce a second hole in the lids of the questionable cans. The test hole was brushed clean of fish discharged by venting steam, flux was applied, and the hole was soldered over. The repaired cans were then sent again to the tester and recooked in the retort. Note the charcoal burner stove on the workbench in the background. One worker is heating a soldering iron in the hearth of the stove.   BCARS 81168

As technology improved in the canning industry, the product was no longer transferred by hand with wicker baskets or pulley conveyances, but placed in wheeled carts like the one in this photo.
BCARS 75295

Trays of processed salmon left to cool in a warehouse.   BCARS 75299

In the early days of salmon canning the cans were not lacquered, and they deteriorated quickly, resulting in spoilage. One early attempt at increasing preservation was to dip the cans in a protective coat of varnish as shown in this photo. In recent years the lacquering of cans has become mandatory. Technology has now produced a can that will not deteriorate and has no body seams that could cause a leak during processing or storage.   BCARS 84150

Boxing the canned salmon in wooden boxes that were made at the cannery sawmill, or one in the area. Here the worker holds the opening of the wooden box against the box-up machine while the machine shunts the cans into the box. The container is then dropped onto a conveyor which takes it away to the shipping area. In recent years cardboard boxes have become standard.   BCARS 75292

Loading a cargo of canned salmon for the export trade at a cannery on the Skeena
River. Workmen load a cargo sling to be taken aboard one of the many coastal
steamers bound for Vancouver. From there the product will be shipped to
Liverpool, England.   BCARS 74582

Salmon canneries, cold storages, and fish meal and reduction plants eventually dotted the British Columbia coast in great numbers. There are 223 known and documented sites. On the Nass River there were eleven plants. In the Prince Rupert area, including Port Simpson and Metlakatla, there were eight. Nineteen canneries were located on the Skeena River, including the Humpback Bay plant on Porcher Island.

Originally all of the plants were isolated way points served only by steamships, tugs, and fishboats. By 1914 the Grand Trunk Pacific Railway (now the Canadian National) had built a line along the Skeena River, with its western terminus in Prince Rupert. This provided the Prince Rupert-Skeena River salmon industry with a new shipping access. But the Nass River canneries remained in total isolation.

For the people of the north coast, the fishing industry was a unique and intensive season that monopolized the summer months. It was unique in that they were cloistered together among a workforce of people from many races and tongues. It was intense because of the nature of the industry, which was not only seasonal but competitive and totally engaged in the acquisition and the preservation of a highly perishable product.

Fishermen came and went, delivering their catches, which had to be processed immediately or held in cold storage in order to maintain quality. There was no percentage in spoilage.

Fishermen required services, such as food, gear, and repairs to their nets and boats. Plant machinery had to be maintained. Except for facilities and parts that might be onsite, services and supplies were far removed, in such places as Vancouver or Victoria, several days' travelling by steamer.

If there was a breakdown of any kind, as was often the case, there was seldom recourse short of ingenuity and invention on the part of the management and crews to repair or replace it.

Eventually communications technology in radiophones, faster ships, and airplanes made it easy to solicit the services of a specialized maintenance crew or engineering expert and to bring in parts and equipment to canneries and fishing fleets at any point along the coast.

In the early days all cannery towns had running water, first by open troughs and then by the standard woodstave systems.

Fuel was wood and coal for both industrial and domestic use. It was later replaced by diesel oil and eventually electricity. Power was supplied by water pressure, then power plants. These were located on site and were operated by diesel and in some cases in later years by electricity. Coal oil lamps, gas lighting and eventually electricity provided essential lighting needs.

Medical emergencies were met by itinerant medical men (sometimes a resident doctor as in the case of Port Essington) or by someone with a propensity toward first aid. Once Prince Rupert was established, plants within its periphery had access to all city amenities.

Cannery housing was usually provided to all employees. Some dwellings were barracks type housing set on pilings over the water, or grouped along boardwalks and supported by a trellis network.

The manager's house and those of the staff were usually single or duplex dwellings, sometimes a little more pretentious.

As canning plants became better established the buildings were whitewashed or painted. Gardens and lawns were planted and tended with pride.

Segregation was an integral part of cannery living. Chinese, Japanese, and Indians were consigned to a designated living area or bunkhouse. For the most part it was the system the occupants desired and found most culturally and linguistically compatible. Even so, across the unmarked boundaries friendships were formed and established, often lasting a lifetime. It was the way of the cannery village.

Social life in a cannery began with the first workers arriving in the spring. Exuberant greetings, renewing of past acquaintances and ascertaining who had, or had not, returned to the workforce took place at the arrival of steamer and fishboat.

Thereafter, the occasional break in the ten to twelve hour work day (sometimes longer and including weekends), or a lull between fish catches, provided time for relaxation, social activities, and sports. The centre of town was the general store and post office. There residents met and exchanged pleasantries or information, for there were no telephones until recent years.

For the early fishermen there was nothing in the way of relaxation and very little diversion beyond verbal exchanges across the water, especially if their gear became entangled.

Mrs. L. J. North of Prince Rupert, daughter of the late Peter Herman (a Port Essington canneryman with many business enterprises) remembered the fishermen in their small open sailboats:

Somewhere from down around Claxton Cannery at the entrance to the Skeena someone, usually an Indian fisherman, would start to sing. It was most often a hymn because that was what they knew best. Other fishermen would join in. Those who did not know the words would hum along, even the Japanese who could not speak English.

We watched them drift up the Skeena past Port Essington on the tide in the long daylight evenings of the north coast. There were coal oil lanterns burning aboard each boat and at the end of the gillnets. And when darkness settled, the fleet, with their lanterns, looked like a floating city.

Those on shore would join in the singing too, so that it was like a giant choir filling up the river. When the boats reached the boundary above Aberdeen Cannery they would turn with the tide and drift downriver, out of sight. It was especially effective on a moonlit night.[13]

This all changed with the advent of larger fishing vessels, better accommodation, and such technological innovations as radio and television.

Many canning plants did not survive long enough to experience the changes that came to the industry. The process of amalgamation and consolidation among fishing companies began in 1902. Plants changed ownership, were closed and abandoned. Larger canneries were built and sometimes older ones rebuilt.

The move was toward consolidation, extended fishing areas, better transportation facilities, and the availability of essential services. Finally only a few canning plants remained as opposed to the proliferation that once existed.

Fisheries patrol vessel the *Clyah* on the Skeena River at the North Pacific Cannery dock. Vessels like this one helped to maintain law and order on the fishing grounds by enforcing protection regulations governing fish catches and escapements of spawning stocks into the rivers. PABC 75516

Neat homes with fenced-in yards and cannery style windows at Claxton Cannery.   BCARS 22729

Claxton Sawmill with the Claxton Cannery behind it. The sawmill provided lumber for construction of housing, cannery buildings, floats, scows, and other structures essential to the community. The sawmill also produced lumber for the construction of boxes used in shipping canned salmon.

The photo shows two coastal steamers, part of the fleet of steamships that serviced the north coast for many years. They brought supplies and services to canneries, logging camps, and small communities along the B.C. coast.

In turn, the products produced at these way points were shipped to distribution points in Vancouver and Victoria via the same steamers.
BCARS 22730

The elevated water line in Port Essington in 1902 was gravity fed from a lake on the hill above the centre house in the photo. The line was supported by scaffolding as it traced its way down the hillside and through the centre of town. The line served the community as well as four canneries, Ladysmith, British American, Skeena, and Skeena Commercial. Once, on a very hot day, there was no water in the line. Upon investigation, the crew found a cub bear curled up in the trough enjoying a respite from the heat and unwittingly blocking off the town's water supply.   BCARS 61192

Summer housing for Indian workers at the North Pacific Cannery. Grouped along a connecting boardwalk, on both sides, the houses were two-room single units with cannery windows and corrugated metal roofs.   AUTHOR 1974

Toilet facilities for the Indian Village at North Pacific Cannery.
AUTHOR 1974

Portland Cannery

Portland Cannery was the most northern fish plant on the coast of British Columbia. It was located on Lots 627 and 628, Cassiar District in Dogfish Bay on Pearce Canal, adjacent to the Alaska/British Columbia border.

In August of 1907 Merrill DesBrisay purchased 76.8 acres of land at a dollar each, certificate of payment Number 435. He deposited eighty dollars for Crown Grant Number 7825/380 in January of 1908 and it was gazetted in December of 1908.

Lot 628 forms part of Indian Reserve Number 42, Nass Agency, containing seventy acres. A further $2.50 an acre was paid in December, 1916, under certificate of payment Number 4147.

Lot 627, which was ninety-seven acres of land, excepting a strip of land one chain in width measured from the high water mark, was Crown Granted to Hamilton William in January of 1908. In May of 1916 a certificate of title was issued to Merrill DesBrisay and Henry Alan Bulivar for this property.

A fish cannery was built on one of these properties, probably Lot 627, in 1917. The plant operated one year and produced a pack of 10,598 cases of salmon.[14]

Employees for that single year of operation were:

Bookkeeper: W. Black
Carpenters: T. Parker, H. Bailey, H. Heighes
Foreman: W. Weaver
Netman: O. Lund
Millwright: J. Christie
Messhouse Cook: Chong Guy
Fireman: A. Kelly
Night Watchman: R. Grady
Retort Man: C. Hollan[15]

In October of 1939 the property reverted to the Crown.

Author's concept drawing of the Portland Cannery, located on the Pearce Canal.

Pacific Northern Cannery

Pacific Northern Cannery was located at Nass Point on Observatory Inlet, District Lot 68, Range 5, Coast District. It was a poor place to build, as the winds were strong both in winter and in summer.

The plant was built in 1902–03, primarily for the coho and pink salmon fishery.

In September of 1891, B.C. Canning Company purchased 132 acres at a dollar an acre. A certificate of payment Number 1939 was made in the amount of eighty dollars. Crown Grant Number 365/66 was issued in January of 1893, having been gazetted in October 1892 and fifty-two dollars remitted for Certificate of Payment Number 2464. The Crown Grant was issued on the property in January of 1893.

The cannery, under the name of Pacific Northern Packing Company, operated two years. In 1903 they canned 5,594 cases of salmon and in 1904 processed 10,502 cases.[16]

In 1905 the plant was sold for lack of capital to John Wallace of Wallace Fisheries. The following year Wallace moved the plant machinery and equipment to the southeast bank of the Nass River, about one mile from the mouth, and named the new plant Arrandale Cannery.

The property on which Pacific Northern Cannery was located reverted to the Crown in June of 1947.

Pacific Northern Cannery 1902 - 1904.

Author's concept drawing of the Pacific Northern Cannery on Observatory Inlet above the Nass River in 1903.

Mill Bay Cannery

The site of the Mill Bay Cannery was District Lot 2, Range 5, Coast District, one-half mile above Fort Point on the Nass River.

1877 — Henry Edward Croasdaile built a plant for the processing of eulachon (a small, oily fish abundant in the Nass River system), which was later abandoned. The following year he constructed a sawmill down river from the plant.

1879 — Croasdaile built a cannery and produced a salmon pack, although no official records were kept until 1881.

1881 — Henry Edward Croasdaile pre-empted 160 acres of land at the Mill Bay site, making a deposit of a dollar an acre. In March of 1883 the property was gazetted, and in November the amount of forty dollars was paid for Certificate of Payment Number 640.

1884 — The property was Crown Granted to Croasdaile in February.

1888 — Mill Bay Cannery was purchased by George James Findlay, John Henry Durham, and John Henry Bradie.

1889 — The cannery was transferred to the B.C. Canning Company. A new plant was built by Drainey and Shotbolt. It was then often referred to as British Columbia Cannery.

1893 — The Federation Brand Salmon Company purchased the property in January.

1904 — The cannery was sold to the Kincolith Packing Company Limited in June. It was then a one-line plant.

1911 — A two-storey cold storage with a capacity of two million pounds was built. It operated by water power.

1912 — The old shingle roof of the Mill Bay Cannery was re-covered with corrugated iron to end the task of snow shoveling every winter. Henry Doyle, owner-manager, had two lakes dammed to create a reservoir of water and piped enough to provide power for operating the cannery and later on the cold storage plant. It also provided electricity for the buildings, replacing the kerosene lighting.

Doyle tore down the 10 × 12 cabins lining the pathway connecting the cannery to all living quarters and replaced them with a large messhouse for the entire white population. This reduced the fire insurance from the highest premium of any British Columbia cannery to the lowest. Thereafter, all new canning plants adopted the Mill Bay model.

Mill Bay was one of the first two canneries to install can-making machinery in British Columbia. They also installed the first conveyance system from the soldering machines to the can loft and from the can loft to the filling tables. Mill Bay also made cans for Arrandale and Cassiar canneries.[17]

1916 — In March the cannery became known as the Kincolith Fisheries Limited.

1918 — Northern British Columbia Fisheries, under R. V. Winch, acquired the property in December. That same year the cold storage plant was closed down.

1923 — Mill Bay Cannery was two storeys high, had an area of 24,968 square feet, and was built on pilings over the Nass River. Canning machinery was an Iron Chink, double

61

fish knife, one filling machine, two clinchers, two exhaust boxes, two double seamers, and a lacquer machine.

There were two lines in the cannery and four steam-heated cooking retorts, constructed of steel and covered with asbestos.

There was a machine shop, blacksmith shop, boat building shed, net storage above the cannery, and a boiler house containing one boiler, which was fired by coal and wood. There was no reduction plant, can-making factory, or cooperage shop at this time.

The superintendent then was W.E. Draney.

1926 — Wallace Fisheries purchased the cannery in January for $45,000 cash.

1927 — The plant was owned by British Columbia Fishing and Packing Company.[18]

1947 — In May, British Columbia Packers Limited took title to the plant under Certificate of Title Number 24563-1.

Mill Bay Cannery was located in a fine harbour. The bunkhouse had fireplaces and was often called the Mill Bay Hotel. The manager's house was one of the most elaborate on the Nass River.

The plant was served by a water system from three dams and three reservoirs.

The steam sawmill was capable of turning out 25,000 feet of lumber per week, providing employment for a number of Nass River people.

The salmon pack figures in the opening year of 1881 were 7,700 cases.[19] The poorest production year was 1903 with 5,994 cases. The peak year was 1928 with 36,487 cases. The final year of operation, 1936, saw 26,958 cases of salmon produced.[20]

FISHERMEN 1894[21]

William McNeill and Dan Pollard
A. Watson and C. Scotteen
John Wesley and J. McMillan
A. Gosnell
E. Sampson and C. Musquiboo
George Ward

Lazerus Moody
Matthew Risk
C. and J. Williams
J. Grandison and Alex Smart
Alex Danes and Jim Wesley
P. Claydock and G. Morrison
R. McMillan and boy
William Jeffreys and George Whitfield
Frank Kadex
Peter Mack and Clax
John Alex and Harley
Robert and J. May
Matthew Naas and Jack Buttons
J. C. Robinson and George Scotteen
S. Wright and D. Woods
J. Weenock and C. Naas
A. Johnson and J. Heywood
M. McKay and Johnnie
C. McKenzie and Bob Sam
Timothy Derrick
Moses Oxidan
B. Welsh and P. Martin
S. Grandison and Naas
Barney Risk and J. Kadex
J. Davis
M. Laws and C. Ward
G. Cook and Dr. Johnson
Umgo
Tom Rice and Cumshap

Average number of fish caught per boat (35 boats) was 1,905.

FISHERMEN 1895[22]

Moses Oxidan and Phillip Whitfield
Johnnie Campbell
Bob Welsh and Frank Martin
William Jefferys and George Whitfield
Andrew Johnson and James Campbell
Matthew Naas and Charles Leper
George Cook and Dr. Johnson
Jim Williams and Charles Twissquiss
Billy Jefferys and Gum Sam
Jim Davis
Mark Frost
Dennis Wood, John Callighan and John Dick
Bob McMillan

62

Stephen Allen and William Fullerton
George Ward and Alex Davies
Henry and Alex Smart
John Alex and Henry Tate
Andrew Naas and Johnny Weenock
Robert May and George Miskeboo
Charles Miskeboo and Bob Sam
Jim Luke and Benjamin Disraeli
Peter Mack and Jennie Jones
Ben and George Haida
Charles Williams and George Shepherd
James Kadex and George Lobbus
Matthew McKay and Johnny Stoat
Charles McKenzie
Barney Risk and John Button
Bennett and Charles Haida
Stephen Grandison and Stephen Wright
Frank Kadex and William Ryan
Umgo and Jeff Nibby
William Hindmarsh and Albert Dan
Jack Gundison and Moses Whon
Charles Morrison
Jim Wesley and Billy Jefferys
Harry Foster and William McDonald
Charles Kratz and John Button Jr.
Paul Pry
Barney Cooper and Peter Beckner
Timothy Derreck
Peter Svengalli

Average number of fish caught per boat (43 boats) was 2,264.

FISHERMEN 1896[23]
_____

Moses Oxidan and Dan Bede
John Campbell
William Jefferys and George Sampson
George Shepher and Gum Sam
Matthew Naas and Alex Smart
Jeff Nibby
Mark Kadex
John Alex and James Scott
Cornelius Scotteen and Matthew Haldane
Robert McMilland
Dennis Woods and P. Svengalli
Bob McMillan
Stephen Allen

Alex Danes and Edward Palmer
Charles Morrison
Andrew Naas and John Weenock
Robert May and Fred Allen
Charles Smith and Harvey Snow
George and Phillip Whitfield
Peter Mack
George Russell and William McNeill
Sam Scotteen and Simon Seymour
James Kadex and George Lobbus
Matthew McKay and James Stoat
B. Risk and John Dick
Louis Stewart and Alfred Chinshoot
John Buttons Sr. and Henry Tate
Umgo
Jim Davis and Charles Naas
William Hindmarsh
John Wesley
Jack Grandison and Jenny Jones
Joal Sewell
Alex Weenong
B. Cooper
Charles Kratz
M. Risk and T. Derrick

Average number of fish caught per boat (37 boats) was 1,550.

FISHERMEN 1897[24]
_____

Moses Oxidan
John McMilland
Daniel Woods
Andrew Naas
Peter Mack
Isaac Watts
Abel Ward
Robert McMillan
Robert Campbell
Fred Allen
George Ward
Sam Scotteen
Alex Danes
Umgo
John Alex
Lum Sam
Stephen Allen
Simon Seymour

Godfray Russell
Phillip Ward
John Buttons
William McNeill
B. Risk
Louis Stewart
Clay Welsh
William Jefferys
James Kadex
Cor Scotteen
Bob Welsh
Matthew McKay
Frank Kadex
Frank Martin
James Wesley
Joel Sewell
Jack Grandison
J.T. Swanson
Tim Derrick
Naas Co-op Co.
Charles Kratz

Average number of fish caught per boat (40 boats) was 2,308.

FISHERMEN 1898[25]

Isaac Watts
Barney Risk and George Williams
Stephen Allen
Umgo
Andrew Naas and Johnny Weenock
J. Alex and J. Watts
Peter Mack
Frank Martin and Joe Joule
Johnny Scotteen
William Jefferys and Bob Wells
John Dick and William Pollard
Robert May and Adam Bede
T. Duncan and Charles Leper
Clayock Welsh
Alex Danes and Matthew Haldane
George Ward and William Martin
Fred Allen
George Palmer and J. Charlie
Sennis Woods and Peter Svengalli
Charles Morrison and Tim McMillan
Abel Ward

Mathias
Simon Seymour
Tim Donzela and Jonathon Donzela
George Palmer
Frank Kadex
Alfred Johnson and William Stewart
Moses McKay
Tom Womiba
Condour
Sim Kowah
Watanabi
Neshimoda
Mankiki
Eshomea
Cato
Harry
George

Average number of fish caught per boat (38 boats) was 1,805.

FISHERMEN 1899[26]

Albert and Martha Welsh
John Wesley and Tom Alexander
Peter Stewart
James Ward
Harry Foster and Percy Barton
Alf and Emma Watson
Nishamoto
Tomboo
Walter Haldane
Isaac and M.A. Watts
Alfred Gurney and Tim Donzela
Robert May and Donald Bruce
Umgo and Mrs. Umgo
William Sutton
Stephen Allen
William Angus
Sam Seymour
Alex Danes and Gum Sam
Frank and Matilda Martin
John Dick and Robert McMillan
J. and Louisa Joule
Luke Nelson and George Kiar
Johnny Stewart and William McDonald
Okie
Abel and Emma Wood

The original Mill Bay Cannery located near Fort Point above the Indian Village of
Kincolith on the Nass River. Under owner-manager Henry Doyle, a leading British Columbia
canneryman, Mill Bay pioneered as one of the most progressive plants on the coast.
BCARS 51477

Peter Mack
Louis and Alfred Stewart
Frank and Yeough Kadex
Sam Stewart
Simon and Bessie Seymour
Tom Duncan and Lucy Martin
Robert and William Lely
Matthew McKay
Johnny Weenock and Charles Leper
Fred and Caroline Allen
Max Collison and Andrew Nelson
Cato
Isaac Gurney

Average number of fish caught per boat (39 boats) was 1,973.

FISHERMEN 1900[27]

Henry Smart
Timothy Derreck
L. Stewart
Fred Allen and Henry Foster
Peter Calder and Arthur Calder
Alex Smart and Gum Sam
William McNeill and George Tate
Matthew McKay
Mark Smith
Charles Alexander
Umgo
Frank Kadex and Geough
Cyprian Smith
Gideon Kadex
Moses Oxidan
Isaac Robinson
Lazarus Moody
Alfred McKay
David Doolan
John Dick
Nath and Alf Robinson
Joe Joule
Frank Martin
Peter Stewart
Dennis Woods and Pike Svengetti
Alfred Watson
Harry Angus
Johnny Weenock
Walter Haldane

Stephen Allen
Simon Seymour
Albert Allen
Matthew Naas and Jacob Tate
Andrew and Arthur Nelson
George Whitney and John Alexander
Peter Mack
David Ven and George Palmer
William Jefferys and Jack Mack
Jonah Stevens and Mark Tate
Solomon Robinson
William Angus
Tom Duncan
George Shepherd and Adam Bede
Silas Robinson and George Kiar
George Ward
Herbert Barton and Tim Donzela
Abel Ward
Matthew Donzela

Average number of fish caught per boat (48 boats) was 2,282.

66

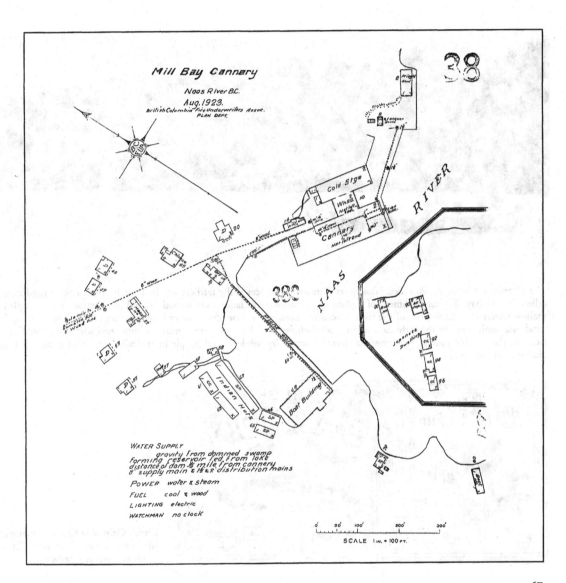

Mill Bay Cannery

Naas River B.C.
Aug. 1923.
British Columbia Fire Underwriters Assoc.
PLAN DEPT.

38

Cold Stge
Whse
Net Loft

Cannery
Net Loft End

NAAS   RIVER

38

Japanese
Dwelling

Indian Hses

Boat Building

WATER SUPPLY
        gravity from dammed swamp
forming reservoir fed from lake
distance of dam ½ mile from cannery
8" supply main & 1½ & 8" distribution mains

POWER   water & steam

FUEL   coal & wood

LIGHTING electric

WATCHMAN no clock

SCALE 1 IN. = 100 FT.

The Croasdaile Cannery, also called Nass River Cannery, was located the farthest up the Nass River at a place the Indian people called Fishery Bay. The establishment of a plant on Indian Reserve lands contravened Federal jurisdiction. That, coupled with the shallow waters and the vagaries of the river, forced the cannery to close after a short three-year operation. The building has no windows, reminiscent of the early days when it was believed that heat and steam must be contained within the building to facilitate the canning process. A sternwheel riverboat stands by, while several people in an Indian canoe on a sandbar pose for the picture.   BCARS 33554

British Columbia Canning Company label used at their Nass River Cannery in 1882.   BCARS 1/BA/SCRL

Croasdaile Cannery

The Croasdaile Cannery was located on Indian Reserve Number 10, Cassiar District, Map 1734, Prince Rupert Land Registry, known as Section 2 and 3, Block 1, Coast District.

1878 — A Crown Grant was issued to J. J. Robertson in July for ten acres of land on the Reserve. In an extract from the Reserve Commissioner's Report dated March 25, 1882, there is a statement confirming Croasdaile's acquisition.

As will be seen from the plan, 10 acres of this flat, almost in the heart of the fishing ground, has been alienated by the local government, a Crown Grant having been issued to Mr. J. J. Robertson on July 22, 1878 which rendered any interference on my part powerless.

This transfer should never have been made, as the land is clearly a portion of the Indian fishing ground. Mr. Croasdaile has since purchased the interest of Mr. Robertson and has built there a salmon cannery and a saw mill.

Adjoining the above land, so alienated, Mr. Grey has erected buildings for the purpose of salting salmon, etc., but inasmuch as he holds no title, I informed him he must remove his buildings, it being my intention to include the land occupied by him in the reservation and I have done so accordingly.[28]

1881 — Croasdaile built a cannery on Indian Reserve No. 10 on the north shore of the Nass River, twelve miles from the mouth.

Mr. Croasdaile received an appropriation of one thousand dollars from the Dominion Government for the removal of snags in the river and the marking of the main channel. He hoped to solve the problem of bringing steamers with less than ten foot draught to the cannery. The work was done by McCullagh.

1884 — The plant was shut down.

1888 — The Croasdaile Cannery was moved to Nass Harbour. The salmon pack for 1881 was 7,700 cases; 1882— 9,600 cases; and 1883/9, 400 cases.[29]

1894 — In March the Croasdaile plant, under the banner of British Columbia Canning Company, was purchased by Walter Morris of the Federation Brand Salmon Canning Company Limited.[30] Under the new owners the cannery operated one year and produced a pack of 8,500 cases of salmon.[31]

An Express Brand canning label printed by the Victoria *Colonist* claimed:

This cannery is situated the farthest north of any in British Columbia and from the very coldness of the waters of the river throughout the summer the salmon partakes of a firmness and delicacy of flavour rarely obtained.

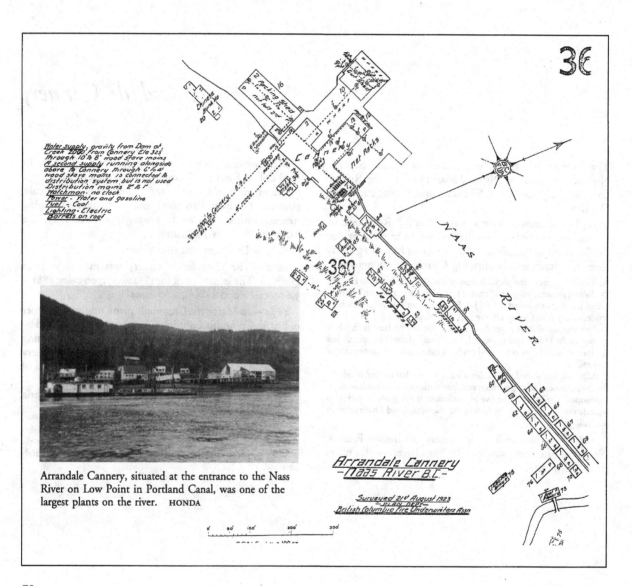

Water supply, gravity from Dam at,
Creek 2000' from Cannery Ele 325'
through 10"to 8" wood stave mains
A second supply running alongside
above to Cannery through 6"to 4"
wood stave mains is connected to
distribution system, but is not used
Distribution mains 2"to 1"
Watchman - no clock
Power - Water and gasoline
Fuel - Coal
Lighting - Electric
Barrels on roof

360

NAAS RIVER

Arrandale Cannery
-Naas River B.C.-

Surveyed 21st August 1923
- PLAN DEPT -
British Columbia Fire Underwriters Assn

Arrandale Cannery, situated at the entrance to the Nass
River on Low Point in Portland Canal, was one of the
largest plants on the river. HONDA

0'   50'   100'   200'   300'

Arrandale Cannery

Arrandale Cannery was located on District Lot 5, Range 5, Coast District at Low Point on Portland Canal near the mouth of the Nass River.

1904 — John Wallace of Wallace Fisheries applied for a Crown Grant on 160 acres of land at Low Point and received it in November. He had previously purchased the Pacific Northern Cannery on Observatory Inlet and now moved it to the new location. Because there was no natural harbour, a rock and log breakwater was built for protection against north winds and winter ice. Fish catches were from Dogfish Bay, Kwinamass River, and the Khutzeymateen areas. Fishermen and plant employees were recruited from the Nass River Indian Villages.

Arrandale was a large cannery complex with one main building fronting the canal and two large buildings along the docks. By 1923 the cannery building was 20,240 square feet and two stories high. There were three canning lines. Machinery consisted of one Iron Chink, two fish knives, one filling machine, three clinchers, three exhaust boxes, and three double seamers. There were six steel, asbestos-covered cooking retorts and one water-power driven lacquer machine.

The boiler house was contained within the cannery. It had two iron stacks thirty-five feet high and was fired by wood and coal. The warehouse consisted of 9,300 square feet. A 1500 square-foot store and office building, a blacksmith shop, and a net storage area were also part of the complex. All buildings were of frame construction and were built on pilings over the water.

There was a good water supply from a dam in the canyon of a creek about one mile from the plant. Water pressure was 135 pounds and most of the plant was run by this power. There was no can-making, cold storage, machine shop, reduction plant, or cooperage. Lighting was provided by a water-power driven dynamo of 7 1/2 kw, 125 volts, 60 amps and 1,000 rpm.

Indian housing was located at the north end of the plant, over the bridge. The seine crew quarters were along the creek, and the Japanese wharf and houses were beyond this point. Management housing was on a hill as was the custom in those days.

1911 — Wallace Fisheries sold Arrandale Cannery to the Anglo-British Columbia Packing Company in February.

Arrandale operated continuously for thirty-eight years. The first season's pack in 1905 was 12,677 cases of salmon. The peak year was 1916 with 41,528 cases, the low year was 1921 with 7,918 cases, and the final year in 1942 saw 17,765 cases produced.[32]

1975 — In August, Impark Holdings of Vancouver and H. G. Jones of Los Angeles, California became the owners of the property.

1978 — Harold Gilbert Jones Jr. of Los Angeles, California became the owner in April.

One of the plant superintendents was W. E. Walker, and a few of the managers were Lord, Young, and Phillipson.

The cannery was also the location of a Fisheries Station, Immigration buildings, and the British Columbia Police force, which served the Nass River area.

The Port Nelson Cannery, like several on the coast, began as a saltery. It was located adjacent to the Arrandale Cannery and was under the same ownership. The two were classified as the same operation for many years.   BELL-IRVING

Port Nelson Cannery

Port Nelson Cannery was located on Lot 198, Range 5, Coast District at Low Point on the Nass River.

British Columbia Fishing Company took out a twenty-one year lease on the property and then assigned it to Port Nelson Canning and Salting Company Limited.

1905 — The Port Nelson Canning and Salting Company built a fish cannery where they had previously operated a saltery.

1910 — In May, a Crown Grant for the property was issued to Port Nelson Canning and Salting Company.

1910 — The cannery and property was sold in December to the Anglo-British Columbia Packing Company of Vancouver, B.C.

1940 — Port Nelson Cannery closed operation sometime in the 1940s, or earlier. Because the Port Nelson Cannery was located adjacent to the Arrandale plant, which closed in 1945, and was under the same ownership, the two plants had long been classified as one operation.

1975 — Impark Holdings Limited in Vancouver and a Los Angeles Lawyer became owners of the property in August.

1978 — In April, Harold Gilbert Jones, Jr., a lawyer in Los Angeles, became full owner.

Because the shoreline was very steep, most of the plant was built over the water. The fresh water supply came from Arrandale Creek, which was shared with Arrandale Cannery, and there were problems over water rights.

In 1905 the main cannery building was 60 × 150 feet with a lean-to for the retorts. A can loft and net loft was con-tained within the same building. There was a saltery, mess-house, Japanese house, China house, store, warehouse, and fish house. A tank sixty feet above the floor of the cannery and situated near the China messhouse had a capacity of two thousand gallons of water.

Machinery consisted of a boiler, one retort, a soldering machine fitted for using coal oil, a combination crimper, one Letson and Burpee capper fitted for half-pound flats and one pound tall cans, one Letson and Burpee wiper fitted for half-pound flats and one pound tall cans, one die press foot, one combination dies for one pound tall cans, one combination dies for half-pound flat cans, two square shears, two hundred standard coolers, one can former, one power fish knife fitted for half-pound flats and one pound talls, fourteen seamer frames, fourteen tall cylinders, four-teen half-flat cylinders, ten seamer fire pots, two bathroom fire pots and one solder pot. The pots were fired by coal oil.

For the first year of canning in 1905 the salmon pack was 10,201 cases. The peak year was 1908 with 15,779 cases. In the poorest and also the final year, 1910, there was a pack of 8,609 cases.[33]

INDIAN FISHERMEN 1905[34]

S. Clayton	Timothy Donally	Paul Sharp
Albert Allen	Herbert Barton	Solomon Bright
D. Watts	Charles Alexander	Charles Yeomans
John Barton	Abel Ward	Richard Morgan
Antone Green	Henry Arzicgh	Alfred Johnson
Joseph Benson	Sol Ward	Henry Wood
John Moore	Jacob Williams	Matthew Lisk
William Lincoln	Arthur Benson	George Ryan

Silas Maxwell   Oscar Johnson   Henry Smith
Stephen Barton   John Wesley   Johnstone Russ
A.M. Watt   Adam D. Joule   Robert Stewart
Peter Stewart   William Smith   Timothy Adams
Donald Bruce   James Robinson   William Sutton
Cornelius Nelson Stephen Allen   C. Smythe

Average fish caught per boat was 1,819.

The Fishing Industry is Everybody's Business

Nass Harbour Cannery

Nass Harbour Cannery was located on Lot 3, Range 5, Coast District, at the entrance to Iceberg Bay, inside the east corner of the cove on the Nass River.

1881 — In October, James Douglas Warren took out a preemption on 160 acres of land at one dollar an acre.

1884 — The Crown Grant for the property was issued in February upon Certificate of Payment Number 679 in the amount of $160.

1887 — In October, James Alexander McLellan bought two-thirds of the property and built a fish cannery there using some of the equipment and materials from the Croasdaile plant on Indian Reserve Number 10. Nass Harbour Cannery was often called McLellan's Cannery.

1893 — The property was sold to the Federation Brand Salmon Canning Company Limited in June. McLellan was one of the principle shareholders in the company.

1904 — In June, the British Columbia Land Investment Agency bought the land and the one-line cannery.

1912 — In July, the plant became the property of British Columbia Packers Association.

1921 — British Columbia Fishing and Packing Company became the owners in January.

1923 — By this year the plant had become a two-line cannery built over the river on pilings and run by steam and water power. Machinery consisted of one fish knife, two clinchers, two exhaust boxes, two double seamers, and a lacquer machine. There were three cooking retorts made of steel construction and steam heated to maintain twenty pounds pressure. The area of the cannery was 16,364 square feet.

Eight feet from the cannery was a boiler house of frame construction situated over pilings. It was fired by coal. There was a store and office of 1,065 square feet, a blacksmith shop, and a freight shed. Residential accommodation consisted of management housing, Indian dwellings, and a Chinese bunkhouse. Lighting was provided by coal oil lamps.

1923 — G. Chambers was manager.

1928 — The cannery closed after operating from 1892 to 1927.

1933 — Wallace Fisheries became the next owners in December.

1940 — The property reverted to the Crown in December. Nass Harbour Cannery was in a good location—a large harbour with fair protection. There was a good water supply and tidal access.

The 1892 salmon pack was 11,250 cases. The poorest pack was in 1903 with 6,127 cases. The peak canning year was 1916 with 20,881 cases. The final year produced 6,572 cases of salmon in 1927.[35]

76

◄ Nass Harbour Cannery was often referred to as McLellan's Cannery. Tucked into a bay at the southern entrance to Iceberg Bay on the Nass River, the plant was in a good location with fair protection. The sternwheel riverboat, *Princess Louise,* is alongside the dock. Two Indian dugout canoes are on the beach.   BCARS 10709

A. J. McLellan built the Nass Harbour Cannery in 1887. For several years he was the major shareholder in the plant as well as its manager.
BCARS I/BA/C67

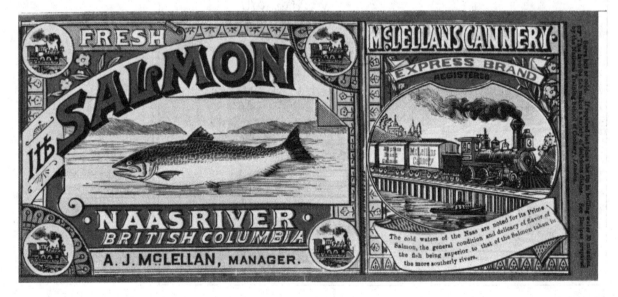

FRESH SALMON
1 lb
•NAAS RIVER•
BRITISH COLUMBIA
A. J. McLELLAN, MANAGER.

McLELLANS CANNERY
EXPRESS BRAND
REGISTERED

The cold waters of the Nass are noted for its Prime Salmon, the general condition and delicacy of flavor of the fish being superior to that of the Salmon taken in the more southerly rivers.

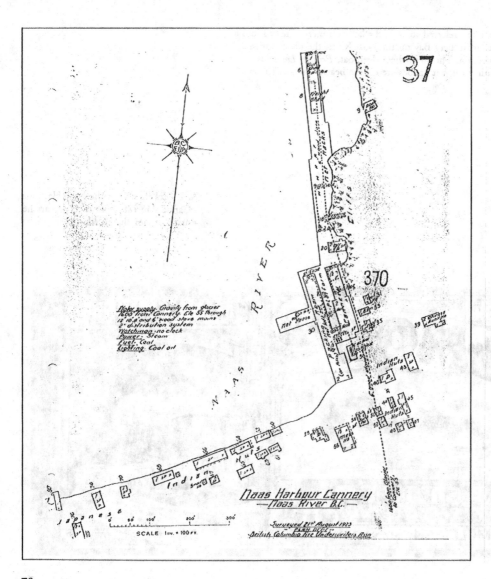

37

370

Water supply: Gravity from glacier
1600 from Cannery. Ele 55 through
12 10,8 and 6" wood stave mains
3" distribution system
Watchman - no clock
Power - Steam
Fuel - Coal
Lighting - Coal oil

NAAS RIVER

Indian Huts

Japanese

Indian Hut

SCALE 1 IN. = 100 FT.

Naas Harbour Cannery
— Naas River B.C. —

Surveyed 21st August 1923
PLANS DEPT.
British Columbia Fire Underwriters Assn

78

The location of Cascade Cannery was in Iceberg Bay on the Nass River. It was built on the southwest corner (1.5 acres) of District Lot 14, Range 5, Coast District.

1888 — The 1.5 acre parcel of land was Crown Granted to William Henry Cooper in December along with Lots 15, 16, and 17 in the same area, a total of 153 acres.

1889 — In August, the southwest portion of Lot 14 was sold to Dennis Reginald Harris.

1889 — Action was commenced in the Supreme Court of British Columbia against Dennis Reginald Harris, Walter Sterling, A. C. Clark, George Hargreaves, Sir Joseph William Trutch, and Samuel Thomas Styles for mortgage payments that were outstanding. The Plaintiff was the Bank of British Columbia.

1889 — The cannery was built by the Cascade Packing Company, beginning with thirty boats and sixty-seven employees.

1893 — The plant was closed.

1900 — A decree was issued in October from the Supreme Court of British Columbia for foreclosure of Lots 15, 16, and 17 Range 5 and part (1.5 acres) of Lot 14, Range 5.

1902 — In June, the British Columbia Packing Association purchased these properties.

1910 — The British Columbia Fishing and Packing Company became owners in May of 1.5 acres of the southwest corner of Lot 14, 151 acres of Lot 15, 76 acres of Lot 16, and 148 acres of Lot 17.

1934 — The property was taken over by the Millerd Packing Company.

1940 — The southwest portion (1.5 acres) reverted to the Crown in October.

Cases of salmon packed were; 1889—4,600; 1890—7,000; 1891—3,000; 1892—7,500, and 1893—4,090.[36]

FISHERMEN 1892[37]

Angus Scotteen
Peter Mack
Robert Moore
Cornelius Scotteen
Robert May
Frank Kadex
Phillip Ward
Jim Williams
Moses Won
Amos Gosnell
John Alick
Henry Smith
Mark Smith
Stephen Grandison
William Jefferys
Bob McMillan
Paul Klatah
George Russ
Billy Bell
Billy Stephens
Robert McMillan
David Doolan
William McNeill
Charles Goosegrease (Josiah Wesley)
Timothy Derrick

Cascade Cannery was sheltered in Echo Cove in the southeast corner of Iceberg Bay at the mouth of the Nass River. Note the barrels on the roof of the cannery, set to contain rainwater. The method was part of the strategy used in the very early days for fire protection. BCARS 51459

Isaac Gurney
Dennis Wood
Tom Naas
James Ward
William Foster
Moses Oxidan
Jim Grey
Ly Tamaru
Charles Morrison
John McCormick
James Wannuck

Average number of fish caught per boat (36 boats) was 2,054.

FISHERMEN 1893[38]

Steve Grandison	Charles Muskaboo	David Doolan
William Jefferys	George Colland	George Shephard
Frank Kadex	Amos Gosling	Tom Naas
Peter Mack	William McNeill	Charles Goosegrease
Jim Williams	John Alick	Billy Bell
Billy Williams	Enoch Woods	Timothy Derrick
Charles McKenzie	Robert May	Robert McMillan
Jim Ward	Bob McMilland	Neashook
George Russ	Dennis Wood	George Ward
C. Scotteen	Moses Whon	Harry Brown
Henry Smith	Moses Oxidan	Alex Stephen
Phillip Ward	Jack Grandison	Charles Angus

Average number of fish caught per boat (38 boats) was 1,200.

Douglas Cannery (Sommerville)

Douglas Cannery was located on Lot 6439, Range 5, Coast District, in a small bay north of the Quinimass River.

1882 — The cannery was built by the Douglas Packing Company on unregistered Crown land.

1883 — The cannery was abandoned at the end of the fishing season.[39]

1918 — In July, British Columbia Fishing and Packing Company took out a twenty-one year lease on thirty-eight acres of Lot 6439.

1918 — A new cannery was built at a cost of approximately ninety thousand dollars by Evans Coleman and Evans, heretofore distributors in the canned salmon indus-

Douglas Cannery was also known as Sommerville Cannery. The plant had a short operating history with only eight years of production.

1/BA/C67.1 #40 (DOUGLAS PACKING)

try rather than owner-operators of a plant. The plant was called Sommerville Cannery. It was a small, modern, well-equipped cannery, and the location was fair, except for a poor water supply. McMillan was manager.

1923 — Francis Millerd leased the plant and it continued under the name of Sommerville Cannery.

1926 — Sommerville Cannery was purchased by Wallace Fisheries and the property, in turn, leased by them.

1926 — The plant was taken over by British Columbia Fishing and Packing Company.

1928 — The British Columbia Fishing and Packing Company was part of a merger of many companies into what became British Columbia Packers Limited in 1928.

1934 — Under B.C. Packers Limited the property was abandoned and the leases left to lapse back to the Provincial Lands Department to be subsequently cancelled. The plant was dismantled and parts of the machinery taken to the Queen Charlotte Islands.

The first year salmon pack for Sommerville in 1918 was 14,317 cases, the poorest year was 1920 with 7,630 cases, and the top year was 1924, the final year, with 38,975 cases.[40]

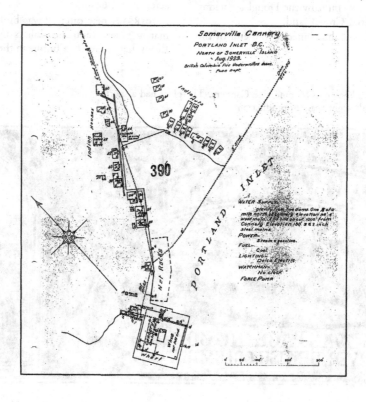

Kumeon Cannery

The Kumeon Cannery was located on District Lot 4954, Range 5, Coast District in Steamer Passage, about two miles south of Khutseymateen Inlet.

1917 — The property was leased by Northern B.C. Fisheries and a cannery built on the site. The venture was based on access to salmon species other than sockeye and good markets secured for coho and pink products in Great Britain.

1921 — The bank for Northern B.C. Fisheries Limited took the company into its own hands when the company was unable to sell an excess stock of canned salmon. Because of such interference, friction, and mismanagement, the Kumeon plant was closed.

The salmon pack for 1918 was 12,000 cases. In 1919 there were 5,595 cases. The final year of 1920 produced a pack of 12,916 cases.[41]

PREVIOUS PAGE:

Installation of a water line at Kumeon Cannery in 1916. Those in the photo, left to right are Henry Doyle Jr.; Henry Doyle, one of British Columbia's leading cannery men at that time; Dick Conteland; and Hal Peck.   SPECIAL COLLECTIONS, UBC

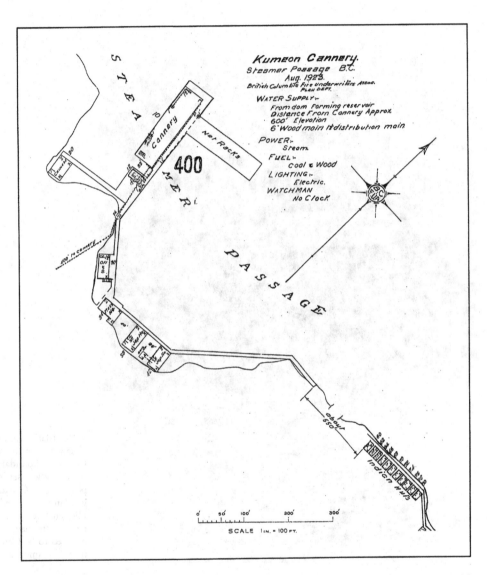

Kumeon Cannery.
Steamer Passage B.C.
Aug. 1923.
British Columbia Fire Underwriters Assoc.
PLAN DEPT.

WATER SUPPLY-
From dam forming reservoir
Distance from Cannery Approx.
600' Elevation
6" Wood main & distribution main

POWER-
Steam.

FUEL-
Coal & Wood

LIGHTING-
Electric.

WATCHMAN
No Clock

400

SCALE 1 IN. = 100 FT.

85

Wales Island Cannery was built by an American firm before the Alaskan-British Columbia boundary was settled. Once the boundary was settled, it was found that the plant was in Canadian territory. The plant was later purchased by the owners of the Hidden Inlet Cannery, which had suffered a reverse fate, having begun in what was believed to be Canadian territory and ended up as an American enterprise. OLSEN

Wales Island Cannery

The Wales Island Cannery was built on Lot 1387, Range 5, Coast District. It was located on Pearce Canal on the west side of Wales Island, about two miles south of Wales Pass. The site was selected because of the pink salmon runs in the Nass River region.

1902 — Wales Island Packing Company Cannery was built by an American firm before the Alaskan boundary was settled.

1903 — Once the boundary between British Columbia and Alaska was established it was found that the Wales Island plant was in Canadian territory. It was then closed down.

1905 — The cannery comprised 12,600 square feet of space with a lean-to shed to house the boiler. Above the cannery was a can and box loft. Machinery consisted of three wooden steam boxes, two Letson and Burpee new style retorts, twelve seamer fire pots and frames using Clarks Kerosene burner system, one Letson and Burpee washer, one rotary crimper, one fish elevator, and about two hundred coolers.

There was a large China house, a messhouse, a store, and two dwellings as well as rows of Indian housing.

The plant had four scows, 14 × 45 feet, with crowned decks; three small scows; one camp scow; three round-bottomed fishboats; and eight seine boats.[42]

1906 — In November, M. W. Boultbee applied for 49.13 acres of land on Lot 1387 at $2.50 per acre.

1910 — The Canadian owners of another Nass River plant, known as Hidden Inlet Cannery, suffered a similar fate but in reverse of the position of the Wales Island Cannery. The boundary placed them within American jurisdiction. Because of this they purchased the Wales Island Cannery and rebuilt it. The firm was Merrill DesBrisay and Company.

DesBrisay replaced almost every pile under the main cannery buildings with mostly five-foot centres in each row. He braced the superstructure, particularly the roof. He upgraded the equipment to two power gang knives, one for talls and one for half-pound cans. He installed two Letson and Burpee washers, both right-handed, one Killington weigher, two Letson and Burpee cappers, one crimper, one Letson and Burpee finger solder machine, two iron steam boxes, and two retorts. As well, DesBrisay added a lathe to the machine shop and a Dynamo for electric lighting. He had a crew of thirty Chinese workers and nineteen Native Indian fillers. Their Jensen filling machine was set to run fifty tins per minute, or five hundred cases in a day.

1911 — In April, M. W. Boultbee paid twenty dollars for Certificate of Title Payment Number 221 and received the Crown Grant for Lot 1387 in September.

1911 — The *Prince Rupert Daily News* stated:

Mr. James DesBrisay has installed a water driven freezing plant and is shipping frozen halibut. He will become a large shipper through Prince Rupert when the Grand Trunk Pacific Railway line is completed. Before Wales Island was ceded to Canada by the Alaskan Award, the DesBrisay family operated the cannery on this island, but after it became Canadian territory the Wales Island salmon pack was declared dutiable in the United States and the cannery was closed. Last year it was re-opened and

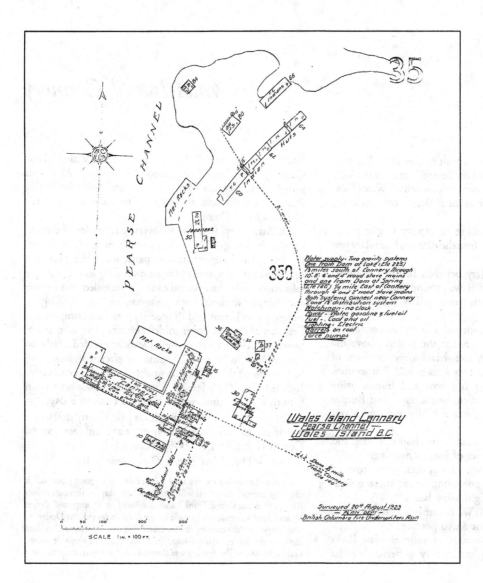

PEARSE CHANNEL

35

Wales Island Cannery
Pearse Channel
Wales Island B.C.

Water supply- Two gravity systems
One from Dam of Lake (Ele 225)
¾ miles south of Cannery through
10" 8" 6" and 4" wood stave mains
and one from Dam of Spring
(Ele 140) ¼ mile East of Cannery
through 4" and 2" wood stave mains
Both systems connect near Cannery
2" and 1" distribution system
Watchman - no clock
Power - Water gasoline & fuel oil
Fuel - Coal and oil
Lighting - Electric
Barrels on roof
Force pumps

Surveyed 20th August 1923
PLAN DEPT
British Columbia Fire Underwriters Assn

SCALE 1 IN. = 100 FT.

88

extensive additions made to the plant. An ammonia freezing plant with a capacity for turning out five tons of ice per day was installed as well as large cold storage rooms for the storage of frozen fish. It is of a direct expansion type, the compressors being an 8 h.p. Armstrong machine.

Halibut caught off Dundas Island are put into cold ovens and frozen stiff. They are carried on racks into the store room and piled like cordwood for shipment in a cold storage steamer.

The plant is driven by water power from a lake in the mountains over the cannery and DesBrisay is engaged in boring a tunnel to augment the water power. In addition DesBrisay had a large salmon pack this year.

1915 — A new Crown Grant was awarded to Merrill DesBrisay and Henry Alan Bulivar on Lot 1387 containing 49.13 acres.

1923 — The cannery building was two stories high, built on pilings over the water and containing 22,000 square feet. There were two canning lines. Machinery consisted of one Iron Chink, two fish knives, two filling machines, two clinchers, two exhaust boxes, two double seamers, and a lacquer machine. Four retorts for cooking were of steel construction, steam heated to maintain ten to twelve pounds of pressure.

The boiler house was located in the cannery building. It was fueled by coal and fuel oil.

Gasoline engines used in the plant were a fifteen horsepower Fairbanks-Morse using suction feed from a sixty gallon fuel oil tank under the floor; a nine horsepower Fairbanks-Morse in the machine shop suction fed from a thirty gallon tank under the floor; a nine horsepower Challenge to operate the canning machinery, which was suction fed from a forty gallon tank below the wharf outside the cannery; and a nine horsepower Neve, which operated the fish haul.

Electricity for lighting was provided for by a 7 1/2 kw, 110 volt Dynamo.

There was no can-making in 1923 but some of the machinery was still there. This consisted of two double seamers, one flanger, and a re-former.

There was a 620 square foot store building, Chinese and Japanese bunkhouses, management housing, and dwellings for Indian employees.

By 1923 there was no cold storage, no can-making, and the plant did not have a reduction plant.

1925 — The Canadian Fishing Company Limited applied for the right to purchase in January. The deed was issued in July.

1931 — The cannery was closed.

1934 — The plant was re-opened

1945 — This was the last canning year, and Wales Island was the last plant to can salmon on the Nass River.

From 1902 to 1913 there were no salmon pack records for the Wales Island Cannery. The peak canning year was 1924 when 46,929 cases of salmon were canned. Other than 1931 and 1943 when there was no production, 1927 was the low year with 7,107 cases canned. The final year, 1949, produced 26,378 cases.[43]

NORTH COAST SOCKEYE SALMON 7¾ OZ. NET WEIGHT | PRESENTED TO COMMEMORATE THE OPENING OF THE PORT SIMPSON FACILITY OF THE PACIFIC NORTH COAST NATIVE CO-OPERATIVE, PORT SIMPSON, B.C. ON OCT. 16, 1975, BY THE PREMIER OF BRITISH COLUMBIA, THE HONOURABLE DAVID BARRETT — PRODUCT OF CANADA | **NORTH COAST SOCKEYE SALMON** 7¾ OZ. NET WEIGHT

Port Simpson can label. GRAY

Port Simpson Cannery

Port Simpson Cannery is located on Indian Reserve Number 2, Range 5, Coast District, at the northern entrance to Chatham Sound, some twenty miles north of the City of Prince Rupert.

1969 — The Pacific North Coast Native Co-operative (PNCNC), formed to establish a fish canning plant on the north coast of British Columbia, proposed to the Federal Government of Canada the establishment of a cannery at Port Simpson. The proposal was turned down.

1972 — The British Columbia Government became interested in the proposal. Under the Social Credit government one million dollars was allocated to ensure a co-operative fish cannery was built at Port Simpson.

1973 — The Provincial Government, under the New Democratic Party, signed an agreement with the Pacific North Coast Native Co-operative, providing an initial three million dollars for the construction of the plant. The agreement was signed by Premier Dave Barrett and President of the Co-operative, Simon Reece. At that time, the Pacific North Coast Native Co-operative, affiliated with the Northcoast District Council, represented five thousand

Port Simpson Cannery, fronting the Indian Village of Port Simpson, is located in a scenic setting. The photo, taken in the winter of 1973, shows the cannery building under construction. The plant was built on an expanded breakwater and land fill in the bay between the island at the left and the main town, behind it. AUTHOR

people on seven Indian Reserves and three thousand people off the Reserves. The government perceived the cannery project as an opportunity for Native fishermen to become economically independent. Their only stipulation was that the government should have a say in who was to manage the plant.

A Board of Directors was set up, representing nine Reserves: Aiyansh; Masset; Skidegate; Kincolith; Port Simpson; Metlakatla; Hartley Bay; Klemtu, and Kitkatla. The first General Manager was Stan Thomas.

1973 — In October construction began on the new plant. An expanded breakwater and land fill was built into the harbour at the foot of the village slope. This accommodated the foundation for a new and fully modern processing plant. Fronting it, an L-shaped dock measuring seventy-two feet in length was installed.

1975 — The dimensions of the cannery were 312 × 150 feet. Two high speed canning lines were installed. The cold storage had a capacity for one million pounds of fish. The reduction plant handling the fish offal measured 75 × 25 feet in area. There was also a large warehouse. Over the plant were spacious office rooms and lunch facilities.

1975 — The plant was officially operating early in March after six years of intensive planning by two men—Stan Thomas and Reg Sampson, with the help of their Board of Directors and government interests. More grants and loans helped expand the plant and establish a gillnet fishing fleet.

1988 — Under the management of the Prince Rupert Fishermen's Co-operative Association, the plant produced 3,000 cases of canned salmon.[44] Since then the cannery has remained closed.

91

Metlakatla Cannery

Metlakatla Cannery was located on Indian Reserve Number Two on the Tsimpsean Peninsula in Venn Passage, approximately six miles west of Prince Rupert.

Metlakatla was an Indian Village founded in 1861 by William Duncan of the Church Missionary Society based in England. His major goal was to instruct and train the aboriginal peoples of the north coast to become morally and economically competent to hold their own in the sudden encroachment of European development and culture.

Duncan insisted that Christianity and the Church become the central influence in the lives of the Native people. From that base he mobilized and expanded economic developments in such trades and industries as blacksmithing, weaving, making bricks, manufacturing products such as soap, tanning hides, and operating their own sawmill to provide lumber for themselves and for marketing. Part of Duncan's plan to develop a stable community was the building and operating of a salmon cannery.

1882 — The Metlakatla Cannery was built on piles along the shoreline in line with a cluster of long sheds housing the sawmill, tannery, printing shop, and the soap and textile factories.

From the outset the plant, known as the Metlakatla Packing Company, had its own gillnet fishing boats and transport vessels. Except for those managing the plant, the cannery was run by the Indian People on a co-operative basis.

1887 — Because of interference from church authorities that, in Duncan's opinion, posed a significant threat to the community's development, almost the entire village of twelve hundred people moved north to Alaska and relocated. They dismantled the cannery and took it with them.

In the three years of operation the cannery produced 5,000 cases of salmon in 1882, 6,871 cases in 1883 and 9,772 cases in 1884.[45]

92

Metlakatla Cannery was the first all-Native Indian salmon canning plant to be constructed, owned, and operated on Reserve lands. Except for management, the plant was run by the Indian people on a co-operative basis. The cannery buildings are located on the lower left side of the photo.   BCARS 55799

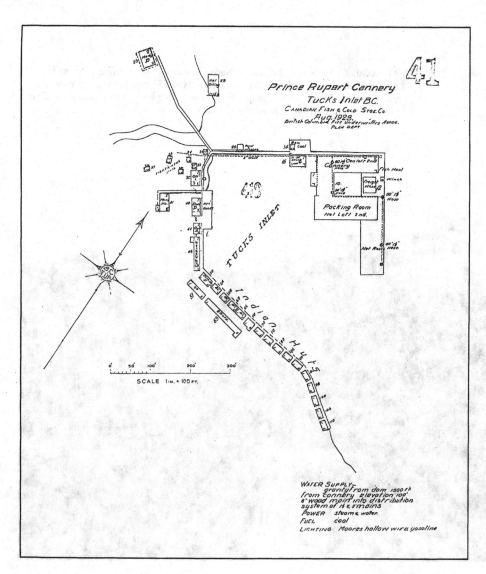

Prince Rupert Cannery
Tucks Inlet B.C.
CANADIAN FISH & COLD STGE.CO.
Aug.1929.
British Columbia Fire Underwriters Assoc.
PLAN DEPT.

47

Cannery

Packing Room
Net Loft 2nd.

TUCKS INLET

Indian Huts

SCALE 1 IN. = 100 FT.

WATER SUPPLY—
gravity from dam 1500 ft
from cannery elevation 100'
8" wood main into distribution
system of 4 & 6 mains
POWER   steam & water
FUEL   coal
LIGHTING Moores hollow wire gasoline

Tuck Inlet Cannery

Tuck Inlet Cannery was located on Lot 541, Range 5, Coast District on the north shore of Tuck Inlet and across from the City of Prince Rupert.

1911 — In June the Atlin Construction Company Limited applied for a Crown Grant on 19.7 acres of land on Lot 541, Range 5, Coast District at a cost of one hundred dollars an acre.

1913 — The property was Crown Granted to the Atlin Construction Company Limited in April, pursuant to an order of the Lieutenant Governor in Council and approved on March 14th. A salmon cannery was built on Lot 541 by the Atlin Construction Company Limited for the Canadian Fish and Cold Storage Company Limited.

Previous to this, the Canadian Fish and Cold Storage Company Limited had built a cold storage plant in the City of Prince Rupert fronting Waterfront Block I of District Lot 251, beginning in 1910 and completing it in 1912. An enthusiastic story in the *Prince Rupert Daily News* described the plant:

Prince Rupert's first industry, construction of a great fish and cold storage at Seal Cove. From April of last year until recently the monthly pay roll of the Atlin Construction Company was a considerable item. Since the offices of Foley, Welch and Stewart, railway contractors, moved from the city last autumn, it has been the only payroll except that of the city.

This is the first industry founded here, the largest of its kind on the continent. Superintendent is George L. Blayton.

The building is huge and windowless, with overhanging eaves and rafters. The lesser buildings have windows. The smoke-stack rises 152 feet (five feet in diameter), constructed of reinforced steel concrete, as are all the rest of the buildings, built on solid rock and having anchor bolts extending into the surrounding solid rock a depth of six feet.

The most modern appliance one sees in the plant is an automatic stoker. The two Babcock & Wilcox improved water tube boilers of 250 horsepower each are fitted with chain grate stokers. There is no firehole, so to speak, for the two boilers. Overhead are two hoppers, or bunkers, which discharge the coal direct on the grates. The bars form an endless chain going over two drums, and the feed and speed at which these grates move can be regulated and it then works automatically. So there is complete combustion and very little of the fuel goes through the big stack in the form of smoke. The size of this boiler room is 42 × 50 feet.

The main building is 80 × 145 feet and six storeys, with two elevators running to each floor. On the first floor are six freezers, each having a capacity of ten tons per day. There is also a room which is called the glazing room. To this room King sockeye, after being properly cleaned is introduced. He is immersed in cold distilled water which forms a coating of ice and this hermetically seals this dainty fish from contact with the common air and enables it to be delivered in London in as fresh a state as when taken from these waters.

Three of the large rooms on this floor are set apart for the use of Prince Rupert merchants, for the cold storage of meats, vegetables and other perishables.

The other five storeys are much the same with rooms of different size for the storage of sea products and also for the storage of eggs, butter and other farm products coming in from Alberta and the Bulkley Valley by train loads as soon as the transcontinental railway begins to run regularly. By then the cold storage plant will be employing 500 men, to say nothing of fishermen.

Adjoining the main building is the engine room, 50 × 80 feet, containing refrigerating machinery of the most modern type and having a capacity of about 150 tons daily. There is also an electric generator, of sufficient capacity to generate all the electricity for lighting and motors the plant can possibly require. On the floor above this engine room is an icemaking room with a capacity of 50 tons of merchantable ice daily.

Next to the engine building is the machine shops occupying 50 × 65 feet in which there is now being installed lathes and tools so the company can make repairs to machinery of the plant as well as gasoline, steam and trawler vessels.

95

Tuck Inlet Cannery, across the harbour from the city of Prince Rupert, was built in conjunction with the Canadian Fish and Cold Storage Plant at the north end of the city. As such they were Prince Rupert's first cannery and cold storage — the latter to become a major facility precipitating the slogan: "Prince Rupert — The Halibut Capital of the World." PAC/PA 95579

The Canadian Fish and Cold Storage Plant as it looked while under construction in September 1911. Built by the Atlin Construction Company, the plant was Prince Rupert's major industry for many years. In 1913 the same company built the cannery at Tuck Inlet, operating the cannery as a subsidiary. They also built the Osborne Cove Reduction Plant on Tuck Inlet. The cannery closed in 1928, and the cold storage plant, under British Columbia Packers Limited, closed in 1982.
SHEPPARD

Mr. G.H. Collins is in England to purchase for the company 15 trawling vessels, 70 feet long with 12 foot beam, schooners with gasoline auxiliary. These will cost $60,000 each.

The plant, by the first of May, will cost about $350,000. The building is fire-proof throughout, the only wood used was for window frames in the lesser buildings; all the lintels are of concrete and the doors specially prepared iron for cold storage buildings, which are imported. The interior walls are a plaster finish, first a layer of hollow tile about five inches, then five inches of compressed granulated cork, one inch of Watsonite, a composition having mastic as its base, then more cork, a layer of hollow tiles and the plaster. The floors are constructed the same way. The building will stand a pressure of 400 pounds to the foot.

The fish storing capacity in the main building will be 13,600,000 pounds in addition to the cold storage rooms for customers. The cold storage rooms can maintain as low a temperature as 25 below zero.[46]

1918 — British Columbia Packers Association operated the across-the-harbour Tuck Inlet Cannery two years.

1920 — The Canadian Fish and Cold Storage Company Limited operated the Tuck Inlet Cannery until 1924.

1923 — Tuck Inlet Cannery was two storeys high and contained 18,500 square feet in area. There were two canning lines for tall, one-pound cans and half-pound flat cans. Machinery consisted of an Iron Chink, fish knife, filling machine, two clinchers, two exhaust boxes, three double seamers, and a lacquer machine. There were two retorts of steel construction steam heated to maintain fifteen pounds pressure. Power was supplied by steam and water.

The boilerhouse was located thirty feet from the cannery and the boiler was fueled by coal. The cannery store and office consisted of nine hundred square feet of space. Other buildings were a blacksmith shop, freight shed, messhouse, manager's dwelling, fishermen's huts, cabins, and housing for Indian workers and their families.

On the site there was no can manufacturing or reduction plant and there were no cold storage facilities. However, there was a reduction plant at Osborne Cove across the harbour from the cannery and also in Tuck Inlet, and the company's own cold storage plant in the city of Prince Rupert.

The manager of the cannery was A. Sutherland.

98

1925 — Tuck Inlet Cannery was operated by the Sommerville Canning Company.

1926 — Millerd Packing Company operated the plant for two years.

1928 — British Columbia Packers operated the cannery. At the end of the season the plant was closed.

1931 — In December the Canadian Fish and Cold Storage Company sold their Tuck Inlet Cannery to the Millerd Packing Company.

1940 — In September the Tuck Inlet Cannery and the 19.7 acres of land reverted to the Crown.

The salmon pack for the first year of operation in 1913 was 9,300 cases, which was also the poorest year. The peak year was 1924 with 34,994 cases and the final year of 1928 saw 13,050 cases canned.[47]

The Canadian Fish and Cold Storage Company Limited merged with British Columbia Packers Limited in 1945. Because of the size and volume of production of the plant, (cold storage), Prince Rupert became known as the halibut capital of the world. In April of 1982 the cold storage plant was closed. Shortly thereafter it was demolished. The last manager of the plant was Allan Sheppard.

Longlining

Seal Cove Cannery began as a clam canning plant. After some controversy that led through the Canadian courts and finally the Privy Council in London, the plant was operated as a salmon cannery.   PAC/PA 47741

Seal Cove Cannery

Seal Cove Cannery was located on the Grand Trunk Pacific Railway (later the Canadian National) on lease numbers 2868 and 2685, fronting Waterfront Blocks H and I, Range 5, Coast District at Seal Cove in the city of Prince Rupert.

1925/26—The Sommerville Canning Company built a clam cannery at Seal Cove.

1927 — The Sommerville Canning Company applied for and received a license to operate a salmon cannery from Provincial Government authorities. However, they did not secure a license from the Dominion Department of Marine and Fisheries.

The Federal Government department charged the Sommerville Canning Company with operating a salmon cannery without a Federal License to do so.

The case was tried in the District Police Court of Vancouver and the company was acquitted. It found that the Dominion Government Department of Fisheries did not have the right to demand an annual fishing license laid down under a section of the Fisheries Act. The Federal authorities appealed and the case went to the British Columbia Supreme Court where it was sustained. The finding was that the Department had overstepped its jurisdiction in the matter of civil rights in British Columbia.

The issue then went to the Supreme Court of Canada and finally to the Privy Council in London where the verdict was again sustained in each case. The ruling was that the Government had no jurisdiction over the fishing industry once the fish were caught.[48]

The case ended in 1929.

1927 — The Millerd Packing Company Limited acquired the Seal Cove plant along with several others on the coast when they became an incorporated company in May.

1943 — Francis Millerd and Company Limited opened a two-line cannery at the Seal Cove plant.

1951 — British Columbia Packers took over operation of the Seal Cove Cannery.[49]

Salmon pack records for the first year of canning in 1943 show 5,162 cases. The peak year was 1948 with 18,495 cases and the final year saw a production 8,742 cases in 1953.[50]

The cannery buildings, docks, and boardwalks were located over the water. A bunkhouse was located on the land behind the plant.

New Oceanside Cannery

B.C. PACKERS PRINCE RUPERT PLANT

The New Oceanside Cannery is located on Waterfront Lots 1 and 2 of Block G, District Lot 1992, Range 5, Coast District in the City of Prince Rupert, B.C.

1973 — Following a massive dock fire of June 6, 1972, at Ocean Dock in Prince Rupert, where the Canadian Fishing Company Limited Oceanside Cannery was destroyed, the Canadian Fishing Company purchased a nine-acre parcel of land in Block G of District Lot 1992, in Prince Rupert.

The firm of Phillips, Barrett, Hillyer, Jones and Company (1969) of Vancouver were engaged to design one of the most modern and technologically efficient salmon canning plants on the coast. Construction on the new facility began immediately.

Plans were to consolidate all sections of the Canadian Fishing Company's enterprises on the north coast. Salmon canning, the reduction of fish meal and oil, herring roe operation, filleting and ground fish industry, and the quick freezing and cold storage would all be under one roof. Their fresh fish and cold storage operation at Atlin Fishery and the Reduction Plant at North Pacific on the Skeena River would then be phased out.

1974 — The New Oceanside Cannery opened with six canning lines: three half-pound can lines, two quarter-pound can lines, and one one-pound tall line. There were three sharp freezers and a cold storage capacity of 110 tons at one filling of the freezers. Two modern unloading stations on the waterfront side of the plant, fresh fish handling facilities, large holding tanks, conveyor systems, comfortable offices, and a large lunch room were all part of the complex.

Managers of the New Oceanside Cannery under the Canadian Fishing Company were successively: Ted Moore, Hank Auchterlone, and Don McLeod.

1980 — The New Oceanside Cannery was purchased by British Columbia Packers Limited. For two seasons B.C. Packers operated both the New Oceanside Cannery and their Port Edward Plant. Consolidation of the two plants was completed in 1981/82, when three quarter-pound, three half-pound, and one one-pound high-speed canning lines were moved to New Oceanside from the Port Edward plant. Two extra lines, a half-pound and a one-pound tall, were placed in reserve for future needs or expansion.

New Oceanside, renamed British Columbia Packers Prince Rupert Plant, has been geared to a salmon pack of ten thousand cases daily with a maximum twelve-hour shift. With a variable line selection (five half-pound, five quarter-pound and one one-pound line) the cannery is capable of meeting immediate customer demands.

J. A. Simpson was Director of Northern Operations for B.C. Packers Prince Rupert Plant; Allan Ronneseth is the present Director. John Atchison was Plant Manager; Tom Coleman is the current Plant Manager.

In 1974, the first year under the Canadian Fishing Company, the salmon pack was 117,548 cases. In their final year before selling the plant in 1979, the pack was 64,419 cases of salmon.[51]

Under B.C. Packers Limited in their first year of operation in 1980, the salmon pack was 88,544 cases. Their 1981 pack was 143,802 cases, and the 1982 pack was 171,507 cases.[52]

Other types of fish processing done at the plant were salmon and herring roe and the filleting, freezing, and storage of groundfish.

The 1985 salmon pack, the largest ever produced by any Canadian salmon cannery, was 515,000 cases of forty-eight pounds. The 1989 pack was 275,000 cases of canned salmon.[53]

The British Columbia Packers Prince Rupert Plant was built as New Oceanside Cannery for the Canadian Fishing Company in 1973. It was built on the former site of the Prince Rupert Drydock. The plant is now the largest salmon cannery in the world.   AUTHOR 1988

Babcock Fisheries Cannery began as a small fish market on the Prince Rupert waterfront. It is now owned and operated by J. S. McMillan Fisheries.
AUTHOR 1988

Babcock Fisheries Cannery

Babcock Fisheries Cannery is located on Area C, Lot 23, Waterfront Block F, Range 5, Coast District in the City of Prince Rupert. This property was leased from the Provincial Government.

1954 — William Babcock purchased a fish market on the waterfront from James Bacon and Bill Shrubsall. He established Babcock Fisheries. A year later W. R. Bingham became a junior partner in the business.

1957 — Babcock and Bingham built the plant into a one-line cannery for half-pound cans and eventually expanded into modern high-speed lines. They also installed a machine for processing gallon cans and a re-form line for re-forming the flattened can-bodies shipped from the factory in Vancouver. During these years they also expanded the docking facilities from 50 feet to 210 feet and built a cold storage freezer plant.

W.R. Bingham was plant manager for fifteen years, staying on with the company until 1969.

1969 — Norman Gobles, an assistant to Bingham in 1968, became manager until 1972.

1972 — The plant was sold to the N. B. Cook Corporation of Vancouver. Bob Morrison became manager until June 1975.

1974 — N. B. Cook Corporation of Vancouver went into receivership in December.

1975 — W.R. Bingham bought the cannery and renamed it Bingham Fisheries Limited.

1976 — Queen Charlotte Fisheries, a subsidiary of Delta Foods in Vancouver, purchased the plant. This company also went into receivership.

1977 — J. S. McMillan took over ownership of the cannery. The new owners installed a quarter-pound line in 1981 to increase the capacity of the plant.

1978 — Gordon Lindquist became manager of the cannery, which again changed names, this time to McMillan Fisheries.

1982 — The McMillan Fisheries Cannery, under J. S. McMillan Company Limited, expanded and developed into a modern plant with a good production record.

The first salmon pack produced by the cannery in 1957 was 5,572 cases. The 1982 salmon pack was 35,140 cases.[54] In 1989 McMillan Fisheries packed 57,000 cases of canned salmon.[55]

McMillan Fisheries has also maintained consistent production in the ground fish and herring roe industries.

Current plant manager is Gordon Nesbitt.

106

Prince Rupert Fisheries Cannery

The Prince Rupert Fisheries Cannery was located on the original Grand Trunk Pacific Lot Number 2977, Waterfront Block E, Range 5, Coast District on the waterfront of the City of Prince Rupert, B.C.

1940 — Nelson Bros. Fisheries leased 3.33 acres of property at the Ocean Dock site and built a salmon cannery. It was a modern plant with four canning lines: two lines for one-pound tall cans, one line for half-pound cans, and one line for quarter-pound cans. That first season the plant processed 85,369 cases of salmon.

1941 — The salmon pack production was 87,080 cases.

1942 — With the establishment of the American Armed Forces on the north coast at the beginning of World War Two, by order of the United States Secretary of War with Canada's consent, the Prince Rupert waterfront was activated as a sub-port of the Seattle Port of Embarkation early

◄ The crew of men that installed machinery for the Canadian Fishing Company at the Old Oceanside plant at Ocean Dock in Prince Rupert. The Canadian Fishing Company took over the plant when the armed forces of World War Two vacated Prince Rupert. Much of the canning machinery was brought in from the Carlisle Cannery on the Skeena River. Those in the photo are, left to right: Doug Browne, Ralph Holte, Bill Hale, W. F. Floyd, Harry McGee, Harold Britten, and Bill Griffith standing in front. WRATHALL

in the year. Among the waterfront properties relinquished for military use was the Prince Rupert Fisheries Cannery.

1942 — Nelson Bros. Fisheries stored their canning machinery aboard scows until a new site was located at Port Edward, south of Prince Rupert, in 1943. That season other canning plants custom-packed the displaced cannery's salmon pack to produce 90,000 cases.

1942 — A massive warehouse complex was built along the waterfront, incorporating the Ocean Dock facility. Adjacent to the cannery, the American Forces built a cold storage plant with 1,000 ton capacity, a marine repair shop, and a watch tower.

1950 — The American Armed Forces relinquished the use of the Ocean Dock facility.

1951 — The Canadian Fishing Company leased the building vacated by Prince Rupert Fisheries and later by World War Two personnel. Machinery for their plant was brought in from their cannery at Carlisle on the Skeena River, which had been closed down in 1950. Some of this machinery had earlier come from the Canadian Fishing Company plant at Haysport, also on the Skeena River. The newly established salmon canning plant, under the Canadian Fishing Company, became known as Oceanside Cannery and eventually as Old Oceanside when a replacement plant was built in 1974 in Prince Rupert, after the first plant had burned.

1955 — The Canadian Fishing Company purchased Atlin Fisheries, located on Waterfront Block F, leased from

107

the Canadian National Railway. This was not a salmon cannery but a fresh fish and cold storage plant formerly owned by British Columbia Packers Limited, who in turn had purchased the plant from the Northern Fishermen's Cold Storage. (Northern Fishermen's Cold Storage was established by Albert and McCaffery and a group of Prince Rupert fishermen.)

1972 — A massive dock fire on June 6 destroyed the entire Ocean Dock warehousing facility and the Oceanside Cannery. Only the machine shop, net loft, and bunkhouse were saved.

Manager for Prince Rupert Fisheries Cannery, under Nelson Bros. Fisheries, was H. F. Robins.

Managers for the Canadian Fishing Company Ocean-side Plant were Clarence Salter (previously manager of the company's plants of Haysport and Carlisle), Norman Christensen, Billy Malcolm, Johnny Fraser, Ted Moore, and Bill Ross.

Salmon pack figures for the first year of operation in 1951, under Nelson Bros. Fisheries, show 104,689 cases. Their last year, 1941, produced 87,080 cases. Under the Canadian Fishing Company in their first year of 1952, the cannery produced 159,155 cases.[56] The poorest year of operation was 1955 with 52,689.5 cases, and the peak year was 1966 with the production of 198,058.5 cases. The final year's production, 1971, saw 112,660 cases of salmon canned.[57]

The Old Oceanside plant had a small reduction plant. They also processed herring roe for the Japanese market.

Prince Rupert Fisheries Cannery, also known as Old Oceanside, was located at Ocean Dock in the city of Prince Rupert. In 1972 a fire destroyed the cannery and all the warehousing behind it shown in the photo. WRATHALL

Prince Rupert Fishermen's Co-operative

The Prince Rupert Fishermen's Co-operative canning plant is located on part of Waterfront Block A and Waterlot A—Canadian National Railway lease; Waterfront Block 8, Grand Trunk Pacific 2786A and 10327; Parcel A, Government lease; Waterfront Lot 1 Block B—Plan number 3664 Waterfront Lot 2, Block B—Plan number 4423; Block R-1, Part of Block 10 Canadian National lease 10327: all located at Fairview in the city of Prince Rupert.

1928 — The first organized action that would eventually culminate in the formation of the Prince Rupert Fishermen's Co-operative came out of a general fishermen's meeting held in Hunts Inlet on Porcher Island. At the meeting Mike Anderson was chosen and delegated to investigate the merits of forming a cohesive union of some sort. As such, this new association would promote conservation of the fishing industry as well as the interests of the fishermen. Anderson's extensive fact-finding tour of fishermen along the coast led to the conviction that a co-operative was preferable. This resulted in the formation of the Northern B.C. Salmon Fishermen's Association. Out of a number of local meetings, mostly in an old boat house in Seal Cove, the membership established the original Prince Rupert Fishermen's Co-operative Association.

1931 — Prince Rupert Fishermen's Co-operative Association received its official charter on January 21st. The first directors were Gus Norman, president; Charles Lord, secretary; Mike Anderson, Jim Roberts, Leon Sandvar, William Thain, and Sinclair Peyton.

1933 — A discarded city dump scow, with double pontoons, was acquired and made into a fish camp with a store, fish shed, and living quarters. It was stationed at Dundas Island.

1934 — Other collecting stations were placed at Zayas Island, Squadaree, and Banks Island.

1935 — A number of salmon trollers met at Henslung Bay on North Island, adjacent to the Queen Charlotte Islands. Out of a collective agreement for packing their fish to processing plants, they formed another organization. The new group became the North Island Trollers' Co-operative, receiving their charter on August 13th. Their first directors were: Chris Eden, president; H. M. Hansen, secretary; Olaf Warren, E. H. Crawford, and K. A. Rankin.

1936 — The North Island Trollers Association purchased two 110 foot fish packers—*Hickey* and *Kanawaka*.

1936 — The Prince Rupert Fishermen's Co-operative Association bought the fish packer *Azurite* and in the next year the *Ogden*.

1939 — The two co-operatives amalgamated to form the Prince Rupert Fishermen's Co-operative Association under a new charter on December 1st. Members were L. H. C. Phillips, J. Enes, F. Keith, O. P. Warren, M. Berg, R. Nakken, D. Crocker, N. Ruud, W. J. H. Dean, H. A. Newson J. Knudsen, M. Fladset, L. Jacobson, and C. Eden.

1940 — The Prince Rupert Fishermen's Credit Union was formed in support of the financial needs of the Co-op members.

1941 — The Co-op established a fish liver plant on the Provincial Government fish wharf. This serviced seventy-four boats of the Co-op's halibut fishermen.

The Prince Rupert Fishermen's Co-operative Association Cannery complex is located at
Fairview, the south part of the city of Prince Rupert. The plant is a graphic testament to
the strength and purpose of the co-operative system. AUTHOR 1973

1943 — The PRFCA built a fish dock, fish shed and
storage plant at Fairview in Prince Rupert, south of the
main city centre and along the Canadian National Railway.
For a time, ice for the storage plant was brought in from
Lake Kathlyn at Smithers. The Co-op built ice houses there
and cut natural ice from the lake during the winter. It was
shipped to their plant in Prince Rupert by rail.

1945/47—A cold storage plant, ice plant, and liver plant
were built. Thus in a brief period the Co-operative changed
from the status of a local collecting organization, selling
their fish catches to other plants, to an established processing industry.

1947 — A new smoke-house was built, replacing an old
one located above the railway track.

1947 — The Co-op plant received electrical power via
the city of Prince Rupert.

1949/50—The plant was linked by road to the city.

1955 — A fish meal and oil reduction plant was added to
the complex.

1961 — A plant built for the canning of crabs quickly
evolved into an expanded salmon canning plant.

1966 — Docking facilities were extended to increase the
plant's capacity. Three sharp freezers were added to the
cold storage division.

1968 — A new cold storage plant brought that facility up
to a capacity of ten million pounds.

1975/78—A major period of rebuilding and moderniza-
tion took place within the complex with the building of a
new reduction plant, and an ice plant and the renovations
of the filleting plant.

The Prince Rupert Fishermen's Co-operative plant produced their first salmon pack in 1962. In their best canning
season, 1977, they canned 60,400 cases. The poorest year
was 1969 with 6,465 cases. The 1982 salmon pack was
34,750 cases, and in 1989 81,500 cases of canned salmon
were packed.[58]

Jack Deane served as manager of the plant from 1943–
1944; Bill Brett from 1944–45; Ted Sorensen from 1945–
46; and on January 1, 1947 Ken Harding took over as
manager.[59]

Currently Paddy Greene is Chief Executive Officer of
the Prince Rupert Fishermen's Co-operative Association,
and Robert Strand is Plant Manager.

110

Port Edward Cannery

The Port Edward Cannery was located on Blocks 12 and 29 of District Lot 446, Range 5, Coast District in Porpoise Harbour, adjacent to the northern entrance to the mouth of the Skeena River. Block 12, the cannery site on the waterfront, contained 4.05 acres, and Block 29, immediately behind it, comprised 5.95 acres of land.

The cannery site was part of an industrial complex planned by entrepreneurs in 1907–08. They hoped to benefit substantially from the construction of a new transcontinental railway to be extended west to a Pacific Coast terminus in northern British Columbia.

Once Kaien Island (Prince Rupert) was officially designated as the terminus, the viability of the Port Edward site waned. In 1910, with intentions of supplying electricity to the new city of Prince Rupert, eight miles away on Kaien Island, Prince Rupert Hydro and Electric Company purchased the property.

1913 — The Port Edward Cannery was built by Port Edward Fisheries Limited.[60]

An excerpt from *British Columbia in the Making* by John Bensley Thornhill, published in 1913, states:

British industrialist Sir George Doughty bought one of the canneries, some land around it, and also 250 acres of land in Porpoise Harbour on the Grand Trunk Pacific Railway, eight miles from Prince Rupert. He has built an oil-refining plant, a saltery and an establishment for the making of fertilizer.

It is likely that Doughty, under a company called B.C. Fisheries, built a fish oil and meal reduction plant at Porpoise Harbour on the strength of an option to purchase the property. However, B.C. Fisheries, of which Doughty was head, went into receivership in December of 1913. With the intervention of World War One, the plant, like many other enterprises in the north, was abandoned.

1914 — The Grand Trunk Pacific Railway line was completed, linking Port Edward with its transcontinental service.

1918 — The Port Edward Fisheries plant was purchased by Northern B.C. Fisheries, who acquired Blocks 12 and 29. They established a cannery and processed a salmon pack.

1918 — In December, Northern B.C. Fisheries purchased two part 0.18 acres and 0.30 acres of Lot 4476, Range 5, Coast District, property adjacent to their holdings.

1923 — The cannery consisted of 14,850 square feet and was two storeys high. It was a one-line plant with a fish knife, clincher, exhaust box, double seamer, and washing and lacquer machines. There were three retorts of steel construction, steam heated to maintain ten pounds pressure. The plant was operated by water power with steam used for the cooking retorts only.

The boiler house was located thirty-five feet from the cannery. It was fueled by coal. Blacksmithing consisted of a portable forge. There was a brick furnace used for lead melting in the spring (for making leadline to attach to the gillnets.)

A 1,540 square foot store was of iron clad construction and also contained the cannery office.

Port Edward Cannery was an isolated plant about ten miles south of Prince Rupert. During World War Two the American Armed Forces military built a camp around the cannery the size of a small city and housed, fed, and supplied with Arctic clothing and equipment thousands of troops and civilians moving to and from Alaska. They built a road linking Port Edward to Highway 16, and to Prince Rupert. The photo shows on the left a concrete building which was erected by the Prince Rupert Hydro-electric Company in 1910 to house a diesel unit for supplying power to Prince Rupert. Never used for that purpose, the building served as an army barracks, cannery bunkhouse, a temporary recreation facility, and a warehouse.
SPECIAL COLLECTION, UBC

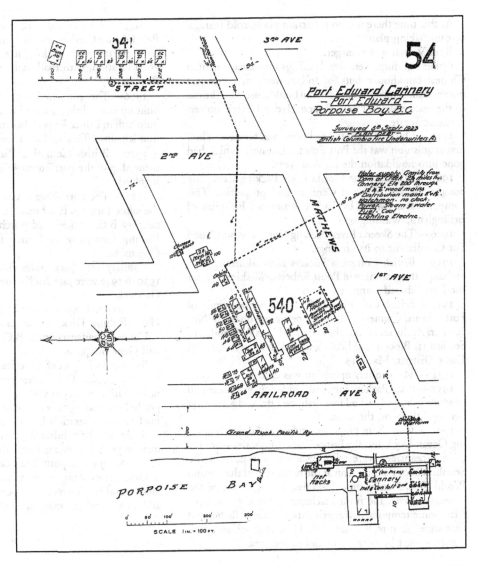

Port Edward Cannery
— Port Edward —
Porpoise Bay, B.C.

Surveyed 5th Sept. 1923
— PLAN DEPT —
British Columbia Fire Underwriters As.

Water supply. Gravity from
Dam at creek 2½ miles fro
Cannery. Ele 200' through
6 & 8" wood mains
Distribution mains 6"&
10 & 12" Distribution mains 6"&
Watchman. no clock.
Power. Steam & water
Fuel. Coal
Lighting Electric

3RD AVE

54

STREET

2ND AVE

MATHEWS

1ST AVE

540

RAILROAD AVE

Grand Trunk Pacific Ry.

PORPOISE BAY

net Racks

Cannery

SCALE 1 IN. = 100 FT.

At this time there was no reduction plant, cold storage, or can-making plant.

R. F. Winch was manager.

Other buildings were five dwellings for management, a Chinese bunkhouse, huts for Indian workers, a Japanese house, cabins, messhouse, a general bunkhouse, and the use of the uncompleted Prince Rupert Hydro-Electric powerhouse structure.

1923 — Queen Charlotte Fisheries was formed. Their first acquisition was the Port Edward Cannery, which had gone into liquidation the previous year.

1925 — In March the Skeena River Packing Company bought the Port Edward Cannery and properties. This company was owned by Pacific American Fisheries of Bellingham, Washington.

1926 — The Skeena River Packing Company purchased Lot C, adjacent to its holdings.

1930 — British Columbia Packers Limited arranged to exchange their cannery in Point Roberts, Washington, for the Port Edward Cannery.

1934 — British Columbia Packers became the owners of Port Edward Cannery and the properties involved, in November. At the same time they acquired Lots A, B and C of Section 11, Block 1 and Lots 1 and 2 of Lot 4445, Range 5, Coast District, Map 949.

1931 — The cannery operation was closed.

1937 — B.C. Packers installed reduction machinery to produce fish meal and oil from salmon offal and a growing herring fishery on the coast.

1942 — Waterfront properties in Prince Rupert, including Ocean Dock and the Prince Rupert Fisheries Cannery (Old Oceanside) were relinquished as sub-port of the Seattle Port of Embarkation at the beginning of the Second World War. Nelson Bros. Fisheries, having to vacate the cannery, moved the plant machinery onto a giant scow. After some temporary arrangements, the scow, floats, and fleet were taken to Port Edward. Their 1942 salmon pack was processed by other canneries in the area.

1943 — Nelson Bros. Fisheries took possession of the Port Edward Cannery property and installed their machinery from the scow, making it a three-line plant. It was a good location, with road, rail, and water access to Prince Rupert.

1966 — The community of Port Edward, which had built up around the salmon industry and later an adjacent pulp mill in Prince Rupert, became an incorporated village municipality. This included the Port Edward Cannery.

1970 — British Columbia Packers Limited took legal ownership of the Port Edward Cannery and the properties involved.

1981 — The Port Edward Cannery closed at the end of the salmon season. Plant machinery was moved to the new cannery B.C. Packers had purchased from the Canadian Fishing Company in Prince Rupert, known as New Oceanside.

Cannery managers under B.C. Packers Limited from 1930 to 1942 were Jack McKenzie, M. H. McLean, and Bill Garriock.

Cannery managers under Nelson Bros. Fisheries were Harry Robins, Dick Nelson, and Sonny Nelson.

Cannery managers under B.C. Packers were Stu Shelley and Gene Simpson.

Salmon pack figures for the first year of operation in 1918 was 39,535 cases. The poorest year, other than the years of no operation, was 1921 with 3,415 cases.[61] The peak year of production was 1972 with 281,542 cases of salmon. The final year of operation in 1981 produced 248,126 cases.[62]

When the Port Edward plant closed there were three quarter-pound canning lines, three half-pound canning lines, and one one-pound tall canning line.[63]

Other types of processing at the Port Edward plant were: salmon and herring roe, the processing of ground fish, crab, and clams, and the canning and freezing of herring.

Inverness Cannery

Inverness Cannery was located on Section 1, Block 1, part of the Indian Reserve Number 6, Plan 3005, Range 5, Coast District. The site was on the north bank of the northern entrance (Inverness Passage) to the Skeena River. The location was first known as Willaclough (an Indian name meaning "The place of the slides").

1870 — William Woodcock, who had no legal title to the property, had established a public inn and trading post on the site, which he called Woodcock's Landing. This was to accommodate miners and fur traders travelling the Skeena River. There were no settlements between Port (Fort) Simpson, the only town on the north coast, and Hazelton, 180 miles inland on the Skeena River. The place was also known as Skeena Bay and Skeenamouth.

1871 — In August a Crown Grant was issued to Henry Soar on 117.3 acres of land on Section 1, Block 1, Range 5, Coast District.

1874 — In April the land was transferred from Henry Soar to Montague William Tyrwhitt Drake, George James Findlay, and William Wilson, who held it in joint tenancy.

1875 — Colonel Lane from the Columbia River arrived at Woodcock's Landing on board a coastal steamer belonging to the Hudson's Bay Company. He came on behalf of Victoria businessmen to assess the possibilities of establishing a salmon canning plant on the north coast. Lane met Archdeacon W. H. Collison at the Landing, and Collison encouraged him to secure the site for a fish cannery. After successful negotiations with Woodcock, Lane returned to Victoria on the same steamer on which he had come.

1876 — The site was transferred to the ownership of the North Western Commercial Company in March. The company built the first salmon cannery north of the Fraser River and named it Inverness. They began with 40 fish-boats and 225 employees.

1879 — Both the Inverness Cannery and Aberdeen (the second cannery to be built on the north coast and sometimes known as Windsor) changed from canning red spring salmon to sockeye salmon.

1880 — In February there was a transaction from John Herbert Turner to William Richard. In November there was another transaction from William Richard to John Herbert Turner and Henry Coppinger Beeton. Through this the controlling firm of Inverness Cannery became Turner, Beeton and Company. J. E. White was manager. Thomas Hankin (once a business partner with Robert Cunningham) became manager of the plant after White died there in March of 1885. Other plant managers were Stapledon and Bill Skillen.

1893 — On February 11th the Inverness cannery was completely destroyed by fire. It was immediately rebuilt to produce a pack of six thousand cases of salmon that summer.

1896 — The plant had two steam tugs, *Florence* and *Spray*. The *Florence* was skippered by one of the first two native Indian captains holding a master's certificate. He was Herbert Clifton of Metlakatla, who served his time on Bishop Ridley's mission boat to secure a certificate of service.

Inverness Cannery was the first salmon canning plant built in northern British Columbia. As such it was the beginning of 107 years of continuous salmon canning on the Skeena River, a record supported by the adjacent plants of North Pacific, Sunnyside, and Cassiar Cannery.   BCARS 69870

Turner, Beeton and Company of Victoria took over ownership of the Inverness Cannery in 1880, selling it to the J. H. Todd Company in 1902. The artwork of their can label has an icy connotation of the northcoast fishing and canning environment.
BCARS I/BA/C67

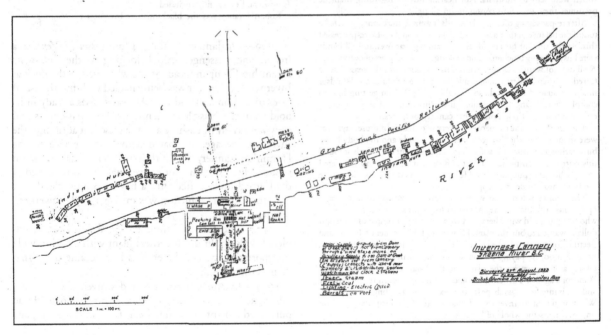

1902 — Inverness Cannery was sold to the J. H. Todd Company.

During the years before Todd purchased the plant there were many difficulties both in ownership and in production. Some of these facts were noted in the Henry Doyle Diaries:

Windsor was in today and I showed him the prospectus of the Skeena River Company and the photograph of the Inverness cannery. He said Neill built the place in 1877 and ran it that season himself having a tinsmith as can-making expert. In the fall of that year he asked Mr. Ewen (a cannery owner on the Fraser River) to recommend some good men as cannery foreman and Mr. Ewen recommended Windsor who at that time was in his employ. Windsor proceeded to Victoria where they had over 2,000 cases of their pack ready to ship. On examining it he found a very heavy percentage of swells and leaks and so had the cases opened and he went over the cans. Out of the lot he finally saved about 1,500 cases which were sent to Australia. Not hearing further regarding them he presumes they went into consumption all right.

After re-packaging these goods Windsor went to the cannery where he found the balance of the pack in a similar condition. He also re-processed this. At the time of his arrival salmon canning was over and all hands were busy canning blueberries and making a very bad mess of everything. Neill did not want to close down on his operations for the season as he feared the shareholders would think the venture a failure, but Windsor finally persuaded him to do so. He also succeeded on getting him to completely re-arrange the canning, discarding nearly all of his machinery, which was entirely unfitted for cannery purposes.

The tinsmith at the cannery was a very poor hand. In those days cans were made so that the lid fitted inside of the body and the body had a burr flaring outwards so as to facilitate lids being put on. Windsor found this burr had been made so that the flare bent inwards and interfered with the lid being put into place. He had to take all these cans and change the burr into the desired shape.

The company lost money on this and the two succeeding years' operations and finally were compelled to go out of business. Windsor, who had remained with them, and who had saved a couple of thousand dollars, wanted to buy the plant. He went to J. H. Turner of Turner and Beeton Company and asked him if he would buy it for him for any sum up to $5,000, he paying $2,000 down and Turner Beeton Company taking a mortgage on the plant for the balance and also acting as Windsor's agents. Turner agreed and told him to return to the cannery and put it into first class shape for the next season, pending the purchase. Windsor stayed at Inverness all that winter (1879/80) and put into improvements the whole of his savings.

Meanwhile the plant was offered for sale by auction and was bought in by some old man in the old country, but subsequently Turner had the sale upset on the ground that as only one bid had been received the sale was invalid. The property was then offered by private tender. At the time of the auction Turner had been authorized by Henry Saunders to buy the property for him, but refrained from making any bid. When tenders were called for he therefore took the matter out of Turner's hands and tendered for the property direct. His bid was $3,000, but Turner put in a bid for $50 more than the highest other tender and although such a tender was not legal he secured the plant on his own account for $3,050. He refused to recognize Windsor in the matter after the season's pack (1880) was up. The latter returned to Victoria, and although the profit on the pack was $15,000 he only allowed Windsor $260 for the time and money the latter had put into the plant in the expectation that Turner was buying the cannery for him.

Windsor did not return to the Skeena but Turner, Beeton and Company continued to operate the plant from the time of purchase until the spring of 1902 when they sold it to Todd for $28,000 — steamer *Florence* and everything included.

Robert Draney was the blacksmith at Inverness in Windsor's first year.[64]

1909 — On January 25 the 154 foot vessel SS *Venture*, a freight and passenger ship belonging to the Boscowitz Steamship Company, caught fire while tied to the dock at Inverness Cannery. It was being loaded with five thousand cases of salmon and had two thousand cases already in its hold from the Nass River canneries. Fifty passengers and crew were safely put ashore and the vessel cut adrift into the Inverness Passage. It floated across on the tide to the Dominion Cannery on Smith Island, posing a threat when it narrowly missed the dock. Eventually what remained of the burned hulk drifted into a bay on Smith Island.

1910 — Robert Johnston was manager of the Inverness, serving there for many years.

1914 — The Grand Trunk Pacific Railway was completed, linking up the Inverness plant with a nation-wide transportation system. Later, this line became the Canadian National Railway.

1920 — In April, a fire again destroyed the cannery, office, nets and supplies, and sixty-two fishboats. Todd purchased a plant from the Green Bay Packing Company in Jarvis Inlet and Robert Johnston rebuilt the plant in time to can 30,526 cases of salmon that summer.[65]

1923 — The cannery had 21,236 square feet of area and was 1 1/2 storeys high. It was built on pilings over the river, at right angles to the flow of the current. Machinery consisted of two fish knives, three clinchers, two exhaust boxes, three double seamers, and a lacquer machine. There were four cooking retorts of steel construction, steam heated to maintain fifteen pounds pressure.

Within the cannery there was a cold storage compartment, which operated on the ammonia system. Refrigerating machinery was driven by a fifteen horsepower semi-diesel engine, fuel oil fed and located in a separate room in the boiler house. The boiler house was located twenty-six feet from the cannery building. It was built of corrugated iron, on pilings, and was fueled by coal.

The plant had a sixteen hundred square foot warehouse, a blacksmith shop and a twelve hundred square foot store and office. Other buildings were housing for management, cabins, Indian housing, Japanese and Chinese bunkhouses, a boathouse, and a church.

There was no canmaking nor reduction plant at Inverness.

1940 — J. H. Todd leased Lot 7443.[66]

1943 — Another fire destroyed the net building and all the nets.[67]

The B.C. Packers Plant at Claxton offered Inverness the use of their net-loft until their new net building could be built.

1946 — J. H. Todd and Sons installed electric power and modern lighting in the cannery complex.

1950 — The Inverness plant was closed after seventy-four years of continuous operation.

1959 — A road was built to the Skeena River canneries of Inverness, Sunnyside, North Pacific, and Cassiar, linking them to Highway 16 into Prince Rupert.

1963 — The Canadian Fishing Company and British Columbia Packers Limited became joint owners of the J. H. Todd and Sons cannery properties, including Inverness. Webb Pierce was manager.

1966 — Inverness Cannery was included in the boundaries of the newly incorporated Village of Port Edward.

1973 — The entire cannery complex was destroyed by fire in October.

1980 — British Columbia Packers Limited received the Certificate of Title to the land.

The first year's canning records in 1877 shows a production of 3,000 cases of salmon. It was also the poorest year. The peak year was 1938 with 62,271 cases. The final year of production in 1950 shows 18,405 cases.[68]

North Pacific Cannery, in its 100-year history, was under the ownership of the
Anglo-British Columbia Packing Company for 77 of those years. North Pacific is
now designated as a site of national historic and architectural importance by the
Historic Sites and Monument Board of Canada. A commemorative placque was
unveiled at the site by Canada Park Service on May 21, 1989, to mark the
occasion.   BCARS 55570

North Pacific Cannery was located on Lot 37, Range 5, Coast District on the north shore of Inverness Passage, the north arm of the Skeena River mouth.

1888 — The North Pacific Canning Company Limited was formed under the *Company Act 1878* in Victoria on November 28, 1888 for twenty-five years. Trustees were Angus Rutherford Johnston, John Alexander Carthew, and Alexander Gilmore McCandless.[69]

1889 — John Alexander Carthew received a Crown Grant of Lot 37, Range 5, Coast District, through a grant in fee of thirty-two dollars for 183 acres of land in December.

1889 — A salmon cannery was built by Carthew and his associates.

1891 — In April John Alexander Carthew sold the plant to Henry Ogle Bell-Irving.

1892 — Henry Ogle Bell-Irving sold the cannery to the Anglo-British Columbia Packing Company. The Anglo-British Columbia Packing Company Limited had been established the previous year by Bell-Irving with Paterson and Company to form a syndicate of British capitalists to purchase and operate several salmon canning plants on the coast of British Columbia.

1900 — William R. Lord was manager of the plant. It was then a one-line cannery. The plant had two rooms for mild cure fish. An eight ton Linde was used to cool the rooms and for keeping the brine cool.

1910 — A cold storage plant was added to the cannery. At that time Victor Larsen was manager.

1912 — Several small shacks were taken over from the construction crews of the Grand Trunk Pacific Railway Company. Located on the North Pacific property, they were moved to the water side of the railway and used to augment the plant's housing.

1914 — The Grand Trunk Pacific Railway Line was completed, linking the Skeena River canneries such as North Pacific to a transcontinental service across the nation.

1918 — A can-making factory was installed. The plant supplied cans to other canneries such as Seymour Inlet, Good Hope, British America, Cassiar, Knight Inlet, Arrandale and Port Nelson.[70]

1920 — The mild cure plant was closed.

1923 — The cannery had an area of 26,024 square feet, was 1 1/2 stories high and located over pilings in the Skeena River. It was a two-line plant, built at right angles to the river with the warehouse and other buildings paralleling the shore. J. E. Lord was manager.

Machinery consisted of an Iron Chink, two fish knives, two clinchers, two exhaust boxes, three double seamers, and a lacquer machine. There were five cooking retorts of steel construction maintaining twenty pounds pressure. The plant was powered by steam, water, gasoline, and fuel oil.

A three-horsepower Gray gasoline engine operated the lacquer machine. One fifteen horsepower Fairbanks-Morse semi-diesel engine operated the fish cannery and the can-making plant.

The cold storage plant was an ammonia system. Refrigerating machinery was belt-driven by steam power.

The boiler house was twenty feet from the cannery. The boiler was fueled by coal. There was also a blacksmith shop.

There was a thirteen hundred square foot store, office, and dwelling combined. Other buildings were a mess-house, several dwellings, Chinese and Japanese bunk-houses, fishermen's quarters, and a large number of Indian houses.

The can-making plant operated in the spring only. Machinery consisted of two slitters, body-maker, flanger, two double seamers, and foot tester. Resin flux was used for soldering in the body-making machine. The solder pot was heated by coal oil.

1936 — The can-making factory was closed.

1936 — A machine shop from the Company's British America Cannery at Port Essington was towed to North Pacific and installed on the dock beside the cannery and warehouse.

1936 — C. E. Avis was manager of the plant.

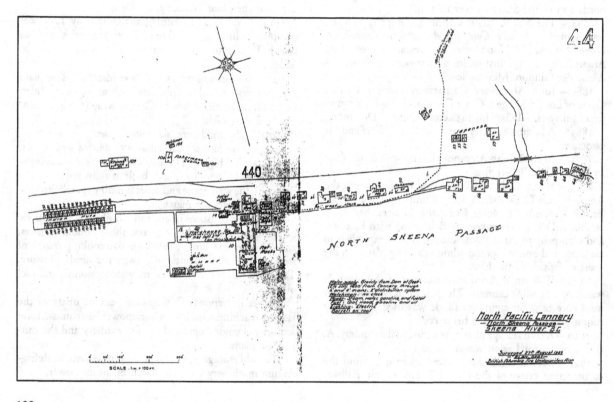

North Pacific Cannery
—North Skeena Passage—
Skeena River B.C.

1937 — Re-form lines were installed upstairs in the cannery. This machinery re-formed flat can bodies, shipped in from a factory in Vancouver, into cylindrical shapes and attached the bottoms to form the base of the cans.

1936 — Collectors and towboats operating out of the plant were the *Tanese, Rose N2, Cape Sun, Haruga, M.Y.*, and the *T.T.* Some were gas powered and some diesel. At that time there was a gillnet fleet of seventy-one gas powered boats and seven still operating under sail and oars. There were four fish scows and one camp scow.

The number of men employed in the cannery was thirteen whites, one Indian, one Japanese, and thirty-four Chinese. Women employed were three whites, thirty-five Indians, and five Japanese. In 1936 there were twenty-nine fishermen owning their own boats for gillnetting. There were forty-eight boat-pullers working among the fleet.

1950 — The Anglo-British Columbia Packing Company Limited leased Water Lot 7497 to expand their operation.

1954 — The cold storage, which consisted of 2,192 square feet, was dismantled.

1955 — A reduction plant for processing fish meal and oil from fish offal and herring was installed.

1959 — A road was built along the Skeena River linking North Pacific Cannery and others to Highway 16.

1966 — North Pacific became part of the Village of Port Edward in its incorporation.

1968 — This was the final year of processing salmon at North Pacific Cannery, except in an emergency in 1972.

1969 — The Canadian Fishing Company Limited became the new owners of North Pacific in January.

1972 — One canning line was restored to the plant to operate for a single season when fire destroyed the Canadian Fishing Company plant at Ocean Dock in Prince Rupert.

1980 — British Columbia Packers Limited purchased the North Pacific plant. Thereafter it continued to operate as a boat station, a repair and maintenance facility, and in the production of fish meal and oil.

Low Prices   Salmon Industry

1981 — The plant was closed.

At its peak, North Pacific Cannery had four canning lines: a quarter-pound line, a one-pound tall line, and two half-pound lines.

The salmon pack figures for the opening year in 1889 was 9,995 cases. The poorest year was 1893 with 7,400 cases.[71]

The final production in 1968 was 31,031 cases of salmon. The incidental year of 1972, when the cannery was reinstated with one canning line to produce a pack for Old Oceanside Cannery, which had burned down on June 6, the salmon pack was 37,195 cases.[72]

North Pacific Cannery operated for eighty years, with the exception of 1905 and 1931 when there was no processing done.

1982 — The cannery buildings are still standing, and the original structure remains incorporated within the existing main building.

Other plant managers who served at North Pacific were Ole Philippson, Keith Philippson, Bill Ross, Mel Hubbel, Hans Winter, and H. Harris.

Tugs and tenders for the gillnet fleet were the *Adam, Eve, Beatrice, Companion, Eagle, Westerner*, and the *G.B. Fairy.*[73]

North Pacific Cannery also produced herring roe for the Japanese markets.

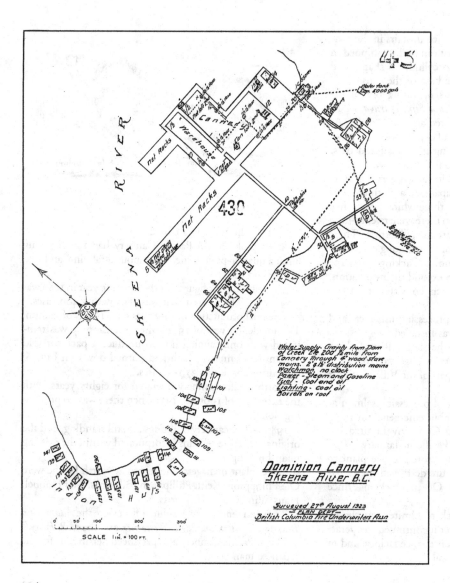

45

SKEENA RIVER

Net Racks

Warehouse

Canned Salmon

Can Loft III

430

Net Racks

Water tank
Cap. 5000 gals

Water Supply - Gravity from Dam
of Creek 2 ½ 200 ½ mile from
Cannery through 4" wood stave
mains. 2"&1½" distribution mains
Watchman - no clock
Power - Steam and Gasoline
Fuel - Coal and oil
Lighting - coal oil
Barrels on roof

Dominion Cannery
Skeena River B.C.

Surveyed 27th August 1923
— PLAN DEPT —
British Columbia Fire Underwriters Assn

0   50'   100'   200'   300'

SCALE 1 IN. = 100 FT.

Dominion Cannery

Dominion Cannery was located on Lot 127, Range 5, Coast district on Smith Island along the Inverness Passage across from the Inverness and North Pacific canneries.

1901 — On June 24th, C. G. Johnston received a twenty-one year lease on thirty-three acres of land on lot 127 at five dollars an acre per annum for the purpose of establishing a fishing station. The lease was issued in the form of the United Canneries of B.C. Limited and gazetted on January 31, 1901.

1905 — A new lease was issued for twenty-one years on the same property on June 24th to George B. Dodwell, Oswald M. Malcolm, Hubert C. H. Cannon and Alexander Stewart.

1906 — The Dominion Cannery was built. Machinery for the plant was brought in from the English Bay Cannery on the south coast.[74]

1909 — The lease on the Dominion Cannery property was assigned to the British Columbia Packers Association by Hubert Cecil Harold Cannon, Alexander Stewart, George Benjamin Dodwell, and Oswald May Malcolm.

1923 — The cannery was 1½ stories high with 19,800 square feet in area. It was a two line plant with one double fish knife, two clinchers, two exhaust boxes, three double seamers and a lacquer machine. There were two cooking retorts of steel construction, steam-heated to maintain twelve pounds pressure. The cannery was powered by steam and gasoline. One four horsepower gasoline Fairbanks Morse engine operated the lacquer machine.

The boiler house was located seventy feet from the cannery. It was constructed of corrugated iron and the boiler was fired by coal. The store was 1,040 square feet with no interior finishing. There was a blacksmith shop, a large warehouse, China bunkhouse, Japanese bunkhouse, manager's house and office, and a number of dwellings for Indian workers and fisherman.

1923 — The owners of Dominion Cannery were British Columbia Fishing and Packing Company. The manager was M. K. Dickinson.

1928 — The British Columbia Fishing and Packing Company was amalgamated with the Gosse Packing Company Limited to form B.C. Packers Limited. Under this new company several canneries on the coast of British Columbia were closed. Among them was the Dominion Plant.

1938 — The lease on Lot 127 was canceled.

The first year salmon pack at Dominion Cannery was 12,001 cases in 1906. The poorest year was 1923 with 1,917 cases. The final year of canning was 1927, when 6,305 cases were produced. There was no production in 1909 and 1925.[75]

One of the gas-powered tugs operating for the Dominion Cannery was the *Klatawa*.

126

◀ Dominion Cannery in a small bay on Smith Island. Its neighbours across the northern arm of the Skeena River (Inverness Passage) are Sunnyside and Cassiar canneries. PAC/PA 47826

Sunnyside Cannery on Inverness Passage, the north arm of the Skeena River, as it looked from the air. Note the water line coming down from the mountain to supply the town with fresh water. WRATHALL

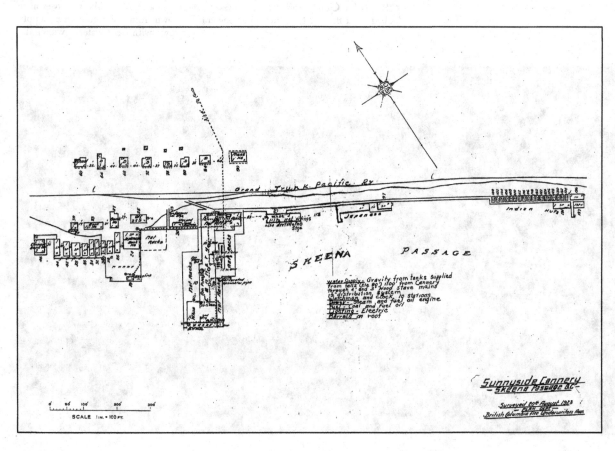

Sunnyside Cannery

Sunnyside Cannery was located on Lot 117, Range 5, Coast District on Inverness Passage, the northern entrance to the Skeena River.

1900 — In February, William Green secured a lease for twenty-one years on 130 acres along the Inverness Passage on Lot 117 to operate a fishing station. He paid twenty-five dollars an acre per annum.

1916 — Robert Cecil Gosse applied for and received a Crown Grant on Lot 117, Range 5, Coast District. Sunnyside Cannery was built under the Gosse-Millerd Packing Company Limited.

1921 — The plant came under the ownership of Gosse-Millard Limited.

1923 — The cannery had an area of 21,300 square feet, and was 1 1/2 storeys high. It was built on pilings over the river, and machinery consisted of an Iron Chink, two fish knives, a filling machine, weighing machine, salter, two exhaust boxes, four double seamers, and a lacquer machine. There were four cooking retorts, steam-heated to maintain twelve pounds of pressure.

There was a blacksmith shop but no cold storage, canmaking, or reduction plants. The boiler was located within the cannery and was fueled by coal.

The store and office comprised 1,300 square feet of space. Other buildings were a Chinese bunkhouse, Japanese bunkhouse, three general bunkhouses, separate dwellings for Japanese families, a messhouse, a warehouse, six dwellings for management, and a number of huts for Indian workers and their families. Later a church and a school were added.

C. F. Strang was manager of Sunnyside Cannery from 1916 to 1930.

1926 — The cannery came under the ownership of the Gosse Packing Company Limited in June.

1934 — British Columbia Packers Limited became the owners of Sunnyside Cannery in December.

1959 — The Department of Highways built a road from Highway 16 to the Skeena River canneries, among them the Sunnyside Plant.

1966 — Sunnyside Cannery became part of the Village of Port Edward when it became incorporated.

Tom Wallace was manager of Sunnyside Cannery for many years. Other managers were Archie Currie and Norman Tarbuck.

In the first year, 1916, the Sunnyside plant's salmon pack was 15,487 cases. The poorest year was 1921 with 15,373 cases.[76]

The final year's production was 95,619 cases of salmon in 1968.[77] Sunnyside Cannery was demolished in 1985/86.

Cassiar Cannery

Cassiar Cannery is located on Lot 44, Range 5, Coast District on Inverness Passage, the north arm of the Skeena River mouth.

1889 — A. E. Green applied for eighty-two acres of land on Lot 44 in December and made a cash deposit of sixteen dollars for Certificate of Payment 3326 in January of 1890.

1890 — The property was Crown Granted to A. E. Green in May, having been gazetted in March of 1890.

1903 — Alfred Eli Green sold the property to the Cassiar Packing Company Limited. Shareholders were D. M. Moore, C.W. Peck, Oscar Brown, A. Wallace, J.S. Scott, and George W. Morrow.[78]

1914 — The Grand Trunk Pacific Railway (now the Canadian National) was completed, linking Cassiar and other Skeena River canneries to rail service across Canada.

1923 — By this year Cassiar Packing Company was owned by Mr. and Mrs. J.M. Macmillan, A. Wallace, and Henry Doyle.

1923 — The Cassiar Cannery was $1^{1}/2$ stories high and contained 16,912 square feet of space. It was built on pilings over the river at the end of a long dock. The plant had two canning lines with an Iron Chink, a fish knife, filling machine, two exhaust boxes, and a lacquer machine. There were three cooking retorts of steel construction which were steam-heated to ten pounds pressure. The boiler house was located thirty-four feet from the cannery and the boiler was fired by coal. The store, office, and post office were 1,360 square feet.

Power for operating the cannery was supplied by steam and gasoline. The plant had electric lighting. Gasoline engines were an eight horsepower Novo to operate the lacquer machine and an eight horsepower Fairbanks-Morse to run the Iron Chink. Blacksmithing was done with a portable forge.

The machine shop was a portable bench with one steam-driven drill.

Housing consisted of four dwellings for Indian employees and separate bunkhouses for Japanese and Chinese workers. Manager of the Cassiar Cannery was J. Lamb.

Eventually Mr. and Mrs. J.M. Macmillan retired, leaving the plant in the hands of their son, Ewen Macmillan. Ewan was a grandson of Alexander Ewen, who built Annieville Cannery on the Fraser River in 1870. Annieville was the first salmon cannery in British Columbia.

1959 — Cassiar Cannery was linked by the new Department of Highways road to Highway 16.

1966 — Cassiar Cannery was included in the incorporation of the Village of Port Edward.

1979 — A cold storage plant with a one-half million pound capacity was built.

1982 — The plant had two quarter-pound lines and one half-pound line.

Cassiar Cannery operated continuously, for eighty years, exceeding all other records on the coast.

The salmon pack for the plant's start-up year in 1903 was 3,401 cases. At its peak in the mid-1960s Cassiar produced 126,000 cases of salmon. The final year's production in 1983 was 90,000 cases.[79]

Some steam tugs used by Cassiar were the *McCullock, Topaz, Linde,* and *Vera.* The *Vera* was a forty-foot flat-bottomed boat brought out from England on a freighter around 1900 to be used in the Yukon. For a while the *Vera* towed fishing boats for Cassiar Cannery. It was eventually beached at Brown's Mill on the Ecstall River.

Other managers of the Cassiar plant were Harry Robins, Herb Glover, Carl Harkness, and Don Macmillan.

130

Cassiar Cannery from the air, shows the cannery complex over the water. Beside it is the machine shop and behind it the powerhouse and several floats. Alongside the highway and the railway is the management housing (at the top of the photo). The messhouse and the office buildings are just above the access road. Below the access road several bunkhouses and Indian dwellings are shown. In neat rows behind the housing are a number of gillnet vessels propped up for winter storage. Later, a cold storage plant was built on the lower side of the access road. BOWMAN

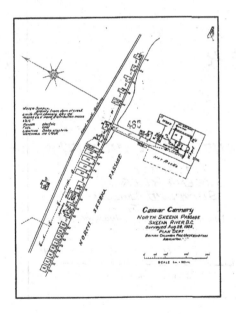

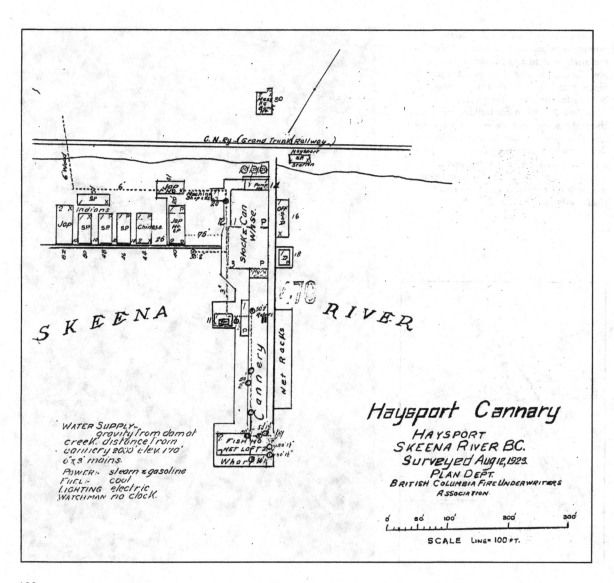

C.N.Ry.(Grand Trunk Railway)

S K E E N A   R I V E R

WATER SUPPLY-
    gravity from dam at
creek. distance from
cannery 2000' elev. 170'
6" & 3" mains.
POWER:- steam & gasoline
FUEL- coal
LIGHTING electric
WATCHMAN no clock.

Cannery

Net Racks

Stock & Can W'hse.

Haysport Cannary
HAYSPORT
SKEENA RIVER B.C.
Surveyed Aug. 12, 1923.
PLAN DEPT.
BRITISH COLUMBIA FIRE UNDERWRITERS
ASSOCIATION.

SCALE LINE = 100 FT.

132

Haysport Cannery

Haysport Cannery was located on Lots 25–29 and 72–76 on Block 10; Lots 58–61 of Block 11; assigned Lot "A" of Block 5 of Lot 4445—all of District Lot 11, Range 5, Coast District in the subdivision of Haysport as laid out in 1909–10. The latter three parcels of Blocks 4 and 5 of Lot 4445 contained 4.75 acres, 4.95 acres, and 3.04 acres, respectively. All properties were located on the north shore of the Skeena River, opposite the town of Port Essington.

1906 — A tentative agreement was made by Frank Enrick to purchase for one thousand dollars four acres of waterfront land at Haysport from Alexander Noble and James S. Adams, who originally bought the land from Turner Beeton and Company of Victoria. The frontage was considered suitable for a salmon cannery because of deep water, proximity to the fishing grounds, and the presence of a fresh-water stream so essential to a canning operation. At that time Enrick had not been aware of plans for the Grand Trunk Pacific Railway line to be built through the property.

1910 — With the establishment of Haysport as a townsite the property owners strengthened their negotiations with the Grand Trunk Pacific for a better deal financially. The railway was not willing to pay.

The dispute went into a court of arbitration in the city of Prince Rupert. The court consisted of Alfred Carss, T. D. Pattullo, and G. R. Naden. L. W. Patmore represented the Haysport townsite company. Fisher and Wharton appeared for the railway, which already had its line under construction through the townsite.

The November 26, 1910 edition of *The Evening Empire* (Prince Rupert) reported:

The Haysport arbitration court resumed proceedings yesterday. The matter in dispute is a block of land on the Skeena somewhere opposite Port Essington which has been laid out and sold as a townsite. One Somerset G. A. Finch of England claims to have purchased 250 feet of foreshore for $32,000.

The case for the townsite company as stated by Mr. Patmore, in council, is that the Grand Trunk Pacific had not established the value of the property—while the G.T.P. claim that as a townsite its value is more enhanced by the presence of the railway.

Lemuel Frere, one of the townsite promoters, who is a broker of Vancouver, said a fish company in which he is interested had made certain proposals to Sir George Doughty relative to the directorate of his company, but Somerset G. A. Finch advised from England that Sir George's terms were too onerous. Consequently the negotiations fell through and Sir George never had any option on any property belonging to this company or their associates on the Skeena.

Lemuel Frere makes the statement that inside of twelve months he will have 100 families of Labrador white fishermen located at Haysport. And Mr. Patmore asserts Premier Laurier and Premier McBride will be bound to take cognizance of the fact.

Mr. Pattullo inquired if this was one of the best sites on the river for a cannery and why it had not been so used.

The witness replied that he had given instructions for all of the 160 acres to be sold and not part.

Lemuel Frere, broker of Vancouver, said he had purchased the land under agreement of sale from Adams and Noble for $17,000. He had received from Somerset G. A. Finch, an Englishman, $5,200 and he expected a payment of $15,000 was now in Vancouver, part payment on the $100,000 purchase price. The payment of this money was arranged—$50,000 stock in a fishing company, one payment of $10,000 and two payments of $20,000.

In answer to a question as to what had created the value of the land the witness (Lemuel Frere) said it was his judgement. The purchaser, Somerset Finch, had spent over $20,000 in this district. Mr. Finch's father was the oldest member of the last British House of Commons and Somerset G. A. Finch would probably be the first mayor of Haysport. The witness was a director on the local advisory board of the Fishing Company of B.C. His company intended to put at Haysport a big cold storage plant, a fertilizer and oilery (reduction plant). He had looked at the place and picked it up as a snap.

G. A. MacNichol said the property at Haysport had an advantage over anything outside of Prince Rupert. He had received offers of purchase from fishing concerns in Seattle and Tacoma, from Mr. Brenton of Vancouver, Dr. Hobbin and C. Jay who used to be with The B.C. Fishing Company, from Harry West and McLean and Ghillis of Vanvouver who were hot after it.

On December 2, 1910, *The Evening Empire* stated:

J. Adams was recalled as a witness. In reply to a question by W.E. Fisher he declared council did not know what he was talking about. The witness would not say whether the fish came past a point lower down the river to get to a point higher up. The council asked did he think the fish came overland. The witness affirmed in fine scorn that council did not know much about fish or he would not have asked that question.

The Evening Empire of December 3, 1910 reported further:

The Haysport arbitration case ended last night and the award is now being considered. The argument in the case by Fisher for the G.T.P. maintained that the land behind the grade at Haysport was marshy and made a poor foundation. He doubted a cannery would ever go there.

Fisher reminded the court that the land purchased for $1,000 had sold for $17,000 to the townsite promoters who then re-sold it to Mr. Finch for a fabulous sum, this value being incidental to the railway.

Further, the townsite plan showed building lots extending out 687 feet at that in 30 feet of water. If they could build streets and houses in 30 feet of water they could also build a cannery.

The purpose of the court was to arrive at the value of the land, not of a fictitious townsite, Mr. Fraser stated.

Mr. Noble said he might be able to get a cannery licence because of his pull with the Dominion Government, but the order-in-counsel regulating these licences had been made in March 1910, and in the time he had held this land he had never obtained a licence, even when there was no restrictions as to their number.

Patmore in summing up his argument desired the arbitrators to vote the association of the land with the foreshore in the conclusion. Getting a cannery licence, Patmore stated, was a matter of influence with the

Dominion Government. Cy Peck had said so. Mr. Adams had for years tried to get Mr. Noble to agree to sell Mr. Ewing a cannery site at Haysport. A cannery at Haysport would mean a saving of $3,500 over any other site on the Skeena.

Patmore continued by stating that Don Moore (manager and part owner in Cassiar Cannery) had said if he had spent $10,000 more at Haysport than Cassiar it would have paid him.

There were many witnesses to the feasibility of Haysport, Patmore pointed out, but the railway grade had covered the rock where the cannery was to be built. A cannery would have to be built below the grade at an increased cost of $2,500. Surely such a man as Somerset G. A. Finch would never forget to take that fact into account.

1913 — A freezer and cold storage plant was built at Haysport by the Maritime Fisheries Limited. The shareholders were Sir Thomas Lipton, C. Williamson Milne, Andrew Weir and D. T. Sandison.

1914 — A new building, 60 feet by 60 feet, was added to the original. It had two sharp freezers 12 × 24 feet each, a glazing room, and two storage rooms all on the ground floor. The capacity of the two twenty-five ton ice machines, one a Linde, was three to four tons of ice daily. Above the main floor were two more floors, but only one was insulated and was divided into two rooms for storage.[80]

Once the two sharp freezers were filled, the surplus (in this case, herring bait) was heaped on the floor in one of the storage rooms. The workers turned it over with a shovel so that the cold could penetrate. The freezing was too slow and the bait had turned sour. However, fishermen complained of the badly cut and broken bait from the rough shoveling.[81]

According to Henry Doyle,[82] Shearer and Draney each claimed to be managers of the plant but were working against each other and the company was suffering losses as a result.

1914 — The Grand Trunk Pacific Railway, a transcontinental line linking Canada from the Pacific to the Atlantic, was completed through Haysport. It later became Canadian National Railway.

1919 — The cold storage plant was made into a salmon cannery by Maritime Fisheries Limited. Aside from the

Haysport Cannery survived in the Skeena River until the fishing boundary was moved ten miles downstream from the original, cutting off productive fishing grounds. The plant was also subjected to the winter flow of ice and the drift logs brought down by high waters in the spring runoff.   BCARS 52936

135

cold storage plant there was a wharf and a hotel at Haysport. The cold storage, as such, had been closed in 1915.

1921 — Maritime Fisheries purchased Lot "A" of Block 4 of Lot 4445, Range 5, Coast District, containing 4.75 acres.

1923 — The Haysport Cannery was a building of two stories high, 11,660 square feet and built out into the flow of the Skeena River, at right angles. It was a one line plant powered by steam and gasoline. Machinery consisted of a fish knife, one clincher, exhaust box, double seamer, lacquer machine, and two cooking retorts of steel construction which were steam heated.

There was a 9,240 square foot warehouse, a 1,200 square foot store, office and dwelling combined, a blacksmith shop, and a machine shop.

Spaced in a row down-river from the cannery, there were bunkhouses for Japanese, Indian, and Chinese workers. On the railway that ran behind the plant was a station.

Manager of the plant was T.A. Sandison.

1925 — Maritime Fisheries became owners of Lots 73–76 of Block 10, Range 5, Coast District.

1926 — In May, Maritime Fisheries purchased Lots 25–29 and Lot 72 of Block 10 and were assigned Lot 'A' of Block 5 of 4445, Range 5, Coast District.

1927 — In December, The Canadian Fish and Cold Storage Company Limited bought Lots 58–61 of Block 11, Range 5, Coast District.

1929 — The New England Fishing Company purchased Lots 58–61 of Block 11 and Lots 25–29 and 72–76 of Block 10, Range 5, Coast District in January.

1932 — Clarence Salter was manager of Haysport Cannery.

In the 1930s the fishing boundary on the Skeena River was moved ten miles down-river from the original. This cut off productive fishing grounds. Salmon canneries above the boundary, such as Haysport, were no longer in a viable position to survive economically.

1938 — The canning machinery, office, and store buildings were put on a scow and towed to the Carlisle Cannery across the Skeena River and outside it's mouth. Clarence Salter was transferred to the Carlisle Cannery as manager.

1980 — All the Haysport Cannery properties were transferred to the Canadian Fishing Company Limited in March.

The first year (and the poorest) salmon pack figures for Haysport were 4,854 cases in 1920. In the peak year 58,235 cases were canned, and the final year was 1937 with 44,078 cases.[83]

Aberdeen Cannery

Aberdeen was the farthest inland cannery on the Skeena. It was located on the north shore of the Skeena River at the mouth of Aberdeen Creek where it joins the river. The property consisted of Sections 4 and 6 of Block 1, Range 5, Coast District, with Sections 7 and 15 added later.

1878 — Crown Grants were issued for Sections 4 and 6, Range 5, Coast District, to Charles Samuel Windsor, William Henry Hetrack Dempster, John Wilson, and Henry Saunders for 157 acres of land and 17 acres as tenants in common. These men built a cannery on the site in the same year and operated it as the Windsor Canning Company (London).

1881 — Section 7, Range 5, Coast District, was Crown Granted to William Hetrack Dempster, John Wilson, and Henry Saunders in December. The section contained forty-nine acres.

1882 — W. H. Dempster was manager of the plant and Alexander McNeill foreman. The winter of 1881–82 was a severe one with a considerable amount of snow.

1883 — Section 15, Range 5, Coast District, containing 160 acres was Crown Granted to William Hetrack Dempster in February. The Section contained forty-nine acres.

1887 — William Henry Dempster sold two-thirds of Section 15, Block 1, Range 5, Coast District, to Henry Saunders in March.

1888 — In November, John Wilson and Charles Samuel Windsor sold their share of Sections 4 and 6 of Block 1, Range 5, Coast District, to Henry Saunders so that Saunders and Dempster became owners for all the properties.

1889 — In March, Henry Saunders and William H. Dempster sold Sections 4, 6, 7, and 15, Range 5, Coast District, to the British Columbia Canning Company.

1895 — The Windsor Cannery (B.C. Canning Company) was destroyed by fire on June 1st with a loss of $50,000 covered by $25,000 insurance.[84] W. H. Dempster was the manager of the plant. It was rebuilt and put out a salmon pack in 1896.

1900/01—F. W. Harris was manager of the cannery.

1902 — A second fire destroyed the cannery. This time it was not rebuilt. To maintain an operation on the north coast the company built another cannery at Oceanic on Smith Island.

1924 — British Columbia Fishing and Packing Company purchased the Aberdeen properties.

1934 — Millerd Packing Company became the new owners.

1939 — The Aberdeen Cannery site reverted to the Crown in June.

The first year salmon pack in 1878 was 3,000 cases. This was also the poorest year. The final year of operation, 1902, was the peak production year with 17,570 cases of salmon.[85]

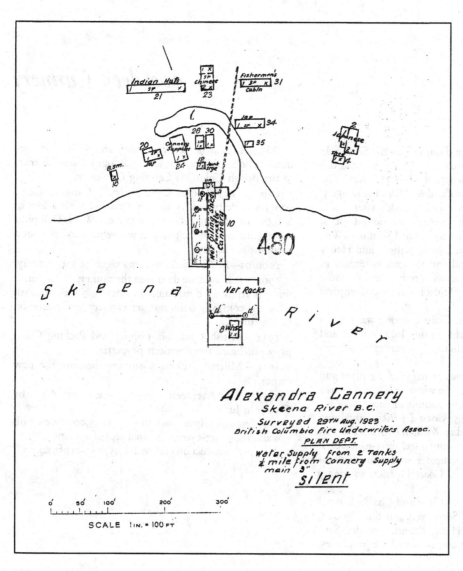

Indian Huts
SP   x
21

1 X
SP
Chinese
23

Fishermen's
1 SP x 31
Cabin

28 30

Cannery Supplies
1 x
24

Jap
1 SP x 34

35

2
Japanese
1 x
Shed x 4

20
x
Jap

12
bunk
srge

B.sm.
10

us

Net Piling Shed
Formerly
Cannery
x
10

480

Net Racks

B whse
x

Alexandra Cannery
Skeena River B.C.
Surveyed 29TH Aug. 1923
British Columbia Fire Underwriters Assoc.
PLAN DEPT.
Water Supply from 2 Tanks
¼ mile from Cannery Supply
main 3"
Silent

S k e e n a   R i v e r

0   50   100'   200'   300'

SCALE 1 IN. = 100 FT

Alexandria Cannery

Alexandria Cannery was located on Lot 53, Range 5, Coast District, close to Carthew Point where the Ecstall and Skeena rivers come together.

1890 — In September Peter Herman applied for a preemption of 166 acres of Crown Land at one dollar an acre. Sixty dollars was paid for preemption record of 315.

1902 — The Crown Grant was issued to Peter Herman in November, having been gazetted in December of 1891.

1902 — Peter Herman sold ten acres of Lot 53, a southerly portion of the property, to Louis Gosnell.

1904 — Louis Gosnell sold the property to the Alexandria Canning Company. This company built the cannery and named the place Alexandria after the daughter of Alexander Ewen. Ewen was a leading pioneer in the establishment of Annieville, the first fish canning plant on the Fraser River. Gosnell stayed on under the new owners to operate the cannery with a full crew of Indian personnel. It was then a one line cannery.

1906 — Robert Kelly and Frank Burnett Sr. purchased the plant.

1908 — The cannery was sold to George W. Cripps.

1909 — In April, George W. Cripps sold out to the Grenville Packing Company, with Mulhall in charge.

1909 — The Grenville Packing Company sold the cannery to Clarence Marpole.

1909 — In October, Clarence Marpole sold to the Kelly Marpole Canning Company Limited. This company changed the name of the plant from Alexandria to Alexandra Cannery.

1910 — The Kelly Marpole Canning Company Limited sold the plant to the British Columbia Packer's Association in May.

1934 — British Columbia Packers Limited purchased the cannery site in December.

1937 — Alexandra Cannery was sold to the Millerd Packing Company in June.

1947 — The property reverted to the Crown in September.

The salmon pack for the first year of canning was 4,335 cases in 1904. The peak year was 1911 with 7,492 cases, and the poorest year was 1906 with 3,048 cases. Figures for the final year of production, 1915, show 7,239 cases of salmon packed.[86]

Balmoral Cannery was located at the mouth of the Ecstall River where it joins the Skeena. The plant grew from a two-line cannery in 1906 to seven lines in 1923.

Mr. J. J. Donaldson, owner of a water-driven sawmill in the area, states that there was an ice-breaker installed on the upper side of the plant. This was to protect it from the river ice in winter. He also remembers there was plenty of deep water, even at low tide, for coastal steamers to tie up to the docks. BOWMAN

140

Balmoral Cannery

Balmoral Cannery was located on Lot 11, Range 5, Coast District, on the north shore of the Ecstall River opposite the town of Port Essington, which was then on the south bank of the Skeena River.

1882 — In September, John Cuthbert took out a pre-emption on 160 acres of land on Lot 11, Range 5, Coast District.

1883 — The cannery was built by John Cuthbert and Richard Stavert Byrn.

1888 — John Cuthbert paid cash in full of $160 for the property in June. It had been gazetted in November of 1884.

1889 — Through the will of John Cuthbert the property was bequeathed to his wife Minnie Cuthbert in January.

1889 — Minnie Cuthbert and Richard Stavert Byrn became tenants in common, or in equal shares, in February.

1897 — L. Conyers became manager of the plant.

1902 — Balmoral Cannery was sold by Minnie Conyers (formerly Cuthbert) and Richard Stavert Byrn to Henry Doyle and Aemelius Jarvis in July. At that time Balmoral was one of the largest plants on the north coast. They had two gas-powered tugs, *Totem* and *Kyak*.

1903 — M. M. English was manager of Balmoral Cannery. At that time there was a packing room beside the cannery, boiler house, blacksmith shop, charcoal house, a large China house for two hundred men, a large Japanese house for seventy men, other Japanese houses each accommodating thirty-five men, fifty-seven Indian houses, and six white men's houses.[87]

1905/06 — The cannery had two canning lines. They also had two steam-powered vessels, called *Pheasant* and *Mount Royal*.

1910 — A cold storage plant was added to the complex.

1911 — A. H. Carter was manager of the plant. There were 115 gillnet vessels fishing for the cannery at that time.

1912/13 — Balmoral Cannery suffered severe damage to buildings and docking facilities from river ice.

1921 — The British Columbia Fishing and Packing Company purchased the plant in January. By then, a large mild cure business (dry-salting spring salmon in five hundred to eight hundred pound tierces or barrels) was established and an icemaking machine was installed at the cannery.

1923 — The area of the cannery was 43,164 square feet. The plant was a seven line cannery with an Iron Chink, three fish knives, one salt machine, two weighing machines, seven clinchers, seven exhaust boxes, twelve double seamers, and one lacquer machine. All were driven by steam. There were six retorts of steel construction, steam heated to maintain ten pounds pressure.

Adjacent to the cannery was a boiler house where coal was used to fire the boiler. Like the cannery, it was built on pilings over the water. There was a 7,200 square foot warehouse, a 2,000 square foot store and office, a net-house of 14,660 square feet of space, a blacksmith shop, and a machine shop. The cold storage plant was contained in the cannery and was steam and water power driven.

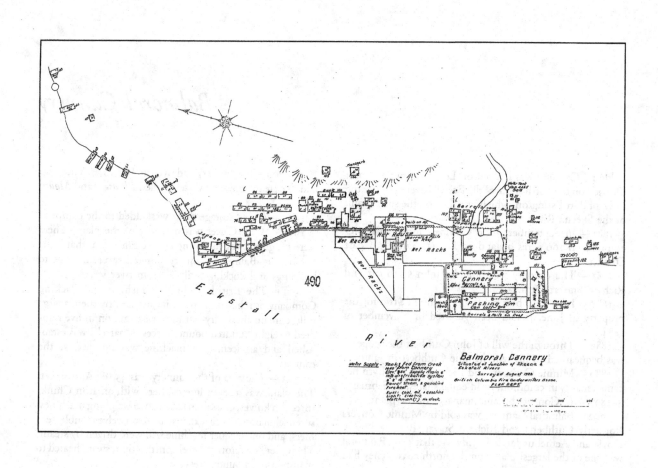

490

Water Supply - Tanks Fed from Creek
near from Cannery
Elev. 350' Supply Main 6"
Instadistributed system
6 x 12 mains
Power Steam, & gasoline
Fire boat
Fuel, coal, oil, & gasoline
Light Electric
Watchman(?) No dock

Balmoral Cannery

Situated at Junction of Skeena &
Eckstall Rivers
Surveyed August 1922
British Columbia Fire Underwriters Assoc.
PLAN DEPT.

Agents for the Balmoral Cannery were Turner, ▶
Beeton, and Company of Victoria.

BCARS I/BA/C67

Can-manufacturing machinery consisted of one slitter, bodymaker, flanger, double seamer, and foot testers. Resin flux was used for soldering in the body-maker machine. The solder pot was heated by coal oil, gravity fed.

Electric lighting was provided by a 14 kilowatt, 110 volt, water-power driven dynamo.

There were several bunkhouses, Indian housing, and management housing. A church was located on the north side of the community.

M. K. Dickinson was manager of the plant. Other plant managers who worked at Balmoral through the years were Marshal English, George Buttermore, and Paul Joseph Cote.

1934 — Balmoral was purchased by British Columbia Packers Limited in December.

1934 — The plant acquired a steam tug called the *Tyee*. In an article written in 1972, Captain Don Peck described this tug:

Balmoral had the colouful *Tyee* which was built for the B.C. Packers and designed on the lines of a war canoe, even to the long overhanging bow carved with the tribal emblem. To compound the felony, they installed an engine in her with the opposite rotation to the normal with the result that she backed to starboard instead of to port when making a landing, so that she was forever sticking her nose in places it had no right to be. By the time she ended her days her snout had been so modified by her various collisions that it was simply a flat surface with very little overhang.[88]

1938 — Millerd Packing Company became the final owners in December.

1944 — Balmoral Cannery and property reverted to the Crown in October.

Salmon pack figures for the opening year in 1883 were 4,173 cases. The peak year of production was 1919 with 52,785 cases, and the poorest year, other than the five sporadic years when there was no canning, was 1893 with 6,372 cases. The final year's output was 15,050 cases in 1933.[89]

Peter Herman

Ladysmith Cannery owner and Port Essington businessman, Peter Herman, was educated to the priesthood in his native Germany but later joined the army. As an escapee from the French troops, he wound up spirited aboard a merchant ship to travel all over the world, eventually ending up at Chemainus on Vancouver Island. He went to Port Essington on the Skeena River, where he worked in a logging camp for the town's founder, Robert Cunningham. He married Kate Spence, daughter of Alexander Spence of Scotland and Victoria. After a two-year stint trapping furs, Herman obtained financial backing to build the Anglo-Alliance Cannery in Port Essington, which later became known as Skeena River Commercial when his partners took over. At the same time he had an interest in the Ladysmith Cannery, which was located on the island adjacent to Port Essington, and also in a sawmill alongside the Alexandra Cannery between Carthew Point and Raspberry Island in the Skeena. It was while Herman, his son, and another man were towing logs to the sawmill that he lost his life by drowning. His foot was caught in the cable used in the towing of the logs and the boat capsized. Peter Herman was then forty-five years of age. NORTH

144

Ladysmith Cannery

Ladysmith Cannery was located on part two of Lot 62, Range 5, Coast District, an island in the confluence of the Ecstall and Skeena rivers. The island was variously known as Ladysmith, Village, or Ecstall. The cannery was located on the south side of the island facing the town of Port Essington.

1892 — The property was Crown Granted to Robert George Johnson.

1900 — John Turnbull built Ladysmith Cannery. That year he produced 724 cases of smoked salmon.

1901 — The property was conveyed to John Turnbull by Robert George Johnson.

Several owners and/or operators emerged in the short history of the Ladysmith cannery; each had vested financial interests in the way of mortgage money.

1901 — The cannery operated under Phillip (Fillip) Jacobsen, who helped to build the plant.

1902 — John Turnbull operated the cannery.

1903 — The cannery was idle. Through an order from the Supreme Court of British Columbia, Fillip Jacobsen became owner of Ladysmith.

1904/05—The cannery was operated by Fillip Jacobsen.

1905 — On June 2, Fillip Jacobsen, by his attorney in fact, Charles Petersen, power, filed No. 2581 to Peter Herman and Kate Herman, joint tenants.

1906 — Under Peter Herman and his wife, the cannery was known as Village Island Canning Company.

1907 — Peter Herman drowned in the Skeena River. In October, the property reverted to the Crown.

A major difficulty in operating the Ladysmith Cannery was in obtaining a supply of fresh water. This was done by running a pipeline from Port Essington underwater to the island.

The peak year of canning was 1906 with 4,181 cases. The poorest year was the final year, 1907, with 206 cases.[90]

The British American Cannery at Port Essington on the Skeena River was built by American interests with American agents located in San Francisco, California. This was their can label before the cannery was taken over by the Anglo-British Columbia Packing Company in 1894. BCARS I/BA/C67

British American Cannery, one of three canning plants built in Port Essington, was known as Boston, B. A., or British American. BCARS 10715

British American Cannery was located on part nine acres of District Lot 45, Range 5, Coast District, at the east end of Port Essington waterfront, close to the confluence of the Ecstall River with the Skeena.

1883 — The British American Cannery was built by Gus Holmes, an American, who with others owned the British American Cannery on the Fraser River. He started with 40 gillnet boats and 225 workers in his plant. Holmes also managed the plant.

1891 — The property was Crown Granted to Robert Cunningham on April 13.

1891 — On April 28, the property was sold to Gustaves Holmes, Benjamin Young, Andrew Young, and John L. Hayseth trading as The British American Packing Company.

1891 — On April 29, Gustaves Holmes, Benjamin Young, Andrew Young, and John L. Hayseth transferred the property to Henry Bell-Irving.

1894 — Henry Bell-Irving transferred ownership of the property to the Anglo-British Columbia Packing Company.

1897 — William R. Lord was manager of the cannery.

1904 — The cannery became a two-line plant.

1909/13 — George Dennstedt was foreman and manager.

1911 — George B. Bailey was manager for a time.

1913/23 — Arthur Kipp was manager.

1923 — The cannery building burned down on May 13. There were 11,119 cases of canned salmon in the fire. The plant was not rebuilt, but moved to the vacated premises of the Skeena River Commercial Cannery located next to it.

1936 — From the Skeena River Commercial Cannery location, the British American canning machinery and machine shop were moved to the North Pacific Cannery on the north shore of the Skeena River mouth, Inverness Passage.

1975 — Ownership of the part nine acres of District Lot 45, Range 5, Coast District was transferred to Impark Holdings of Vancouver and Harold Gilbert Jones Jr. of Los Angeles, California.

The first year of canning, and also the poorest, 1883, saw 5,200 cases of salmon canned. The peak year was 1919 with 39,452 cases. The final year, in the original cannery, was 1923 with 11,119 cases.[91]

In the early days on the north coast, American people were known among the Indian people as Boston men. Canadians, or Englishmen, were called King George men. Under the ownership of Gustaves Holmes, an American, the British American Cannery was called Boston Cannery. After 1900 the plant was referred to as B.A. or British America.

The original Skeena River Commercial Cannery, which began under the name of Anglo-Alliance, was eventually extended to incorporate the two buildings directly in front of it. In 1923 this plant was called B.A. when it was leased by the Anglo-British Columbia Packing Company after their plant burned down.   PAC/PA 21444

Skeena River Commercial Cannery

The Skeena River Commercial Cannery was located on Lots 1–3 of Block 3, District Lot 45, Range 5, Coast District (Map 537) in the town of Port Essington on the south shore of the Skeena River. Later, Lots 1–7 of Block 4 and Lot 8 of Block 2 were added to become part of the cannery, hotel, store, and saloon complex. Skeena River Commercial Cannery was situated between the British American Cannery on the north and Cunningham's Skeena Cannery on the south side.

1897 — Peter Herman with his wife and family moved to Ladysmith Island at Port Essington from Lakelse Lake near Terrace, where he had spent two winters trapping furs. With the money he had saved from working at logging and the fur catches, which included a prize silver fox pelt worth five hundred dollars, Herman went to Vancouver to raise capital to build a salmon cannery, hotel, post office, and saloon at Port Essington.

1898 — Peter Herman purchased Lot 1 of Block 3 from Robert Cunningham in November and built a cannery on pilings fronting the property. His financial backers were the Simon Leiser Company of Victoria. The cannery was first called the Anglo-Alliance.

1899 — Peter Herman built a store and the Caledonia Hotel along the waterfront, adjacent to the cannery. That year Herman, as manager of the cannery, produced a salmon pack for the Anglo-Alliance Canning Company and another for the Globe Canning and Milling Company.[92]

1900 — The plant was known as the Peter Herman Company. That year Herman produced one salmon pack.

1901 — Peter Herman again put up a double pack, this time for Peter Turnbull and for the Peter Herman Company.[93]

1902 — Although there were only three salmon canning plants at Port Essington, the Pearce Cannery is listed as having produced 561 cases of salmon at Port Essington.[94]

According to records, Peter Herman had twice produced two salmon packs in a season (one in 1899 and the second in 1901). For this reason it is likely he also custom packed for the Pearce enterprise.

1902 — Peter Herman, backed by the Simon Leiser Company, purchased Lot 2 of Block 3, District Lot 45, Range 5, Coast District in February.

1903 — The Simon Leiser Company of Victoria foreclosed their mortgages on the Peter Herman Company. At that time assets were the canning plant, wharf and warehouse, thirty-eight fishermen's houses, Herman's residence, Herman's former residence, a butcher shop, hotel building, store, real estate in Port Essington, 140 acres of land at Balmoral, a clam cannery at Dundas Island, the steamer *Mamie*, two scows, three house rafts, a fish camp at a hot springs, a sixty horsepower boiler, a new 1903 engine, China house, and other additional buildings.

Other assets were the Dry Hill Mining Company, Skeena Lumber Company, a logging outfit, and various sundries such as boats, nets, tools, store merchandise, and hotel furnishings.[95]

The foreclosure was in the fall, after Herman had produced a pack of 9,135 cases of salmon.

1904—In April the Skeena River Commercial Company was formed. Its purpose was to acquire the Peter Herman Cannery, hotel, and store. These had been placed on the market by the mortgagors of the properties. The shareholders of the new company purchased the properties for $25,000. W. A. Wadhams, an experienced cannery man and one of the shareholders, became manager of the plant. At that time the cannery was a one-line plant.

1904—In May, the Skeena River Commercial Company purchased Lots 1–5 of Block 4 and Lot 3 of Block 3.

1911—The Skeena River Commercial Company purchased Lot 6 of Block 4.

1918—In December Northern B.C. Fisheries became the owners of the cannery. They took over Lots 1–3 of Block 3 and Lots 1–6 of Block 4. A. D. Matheson was manager of the plant.

1919—Lot 8 of Block 2 and Lot 7 of Block 4 was purchased by the Skeena River Commercial Company.

1923—The cannery consisted of 18,240 square feet and was 1 1/2 storeys high. It was a one line-plant with one fish knife, clincher, exhaust box, double seamer, and lacquer machine. There were three cooking retorts of steel construction, steam heated to maintain ten pounds pressure. Power was supplied by steam, gasoline, and water. The gasoline engine was a six horsepower Simplicity which operated the lacquer machine. For lighting there was a 4 kilowatt, 115 volt, 35 amp Dynamo. The plant had a boiler house situated forty-five feet from the cannery, a black-smith shop, and an office.

There was no cold storage plant, fish offal reduction plant, cooperage, or can-making plant.

1923—The Skeena River Commercial Cannery buildings were leased by the Anglo-British Columbia Packing Company when their British America plant, next door, burned on May 13th.

1925—The cannery property was purchased by the Anglo-British Columbia Packing Company in April. This included Lots 1–3 of Block 3 and Lots 1–7 of Block 4.

1936—The cannery buildings were vacated when the Anglo-British Columbia Packing Company moved their canning machinery and machine shop to the North Pacific Cannery on the north shore of the Skeena River in the Inverness Passage.

1975—Impark Holdings of Vancouver and Harold Gilbert Jones Jr. of Los Angeles, California took ownership of Lots 1–3 of Block 3, Lots 1–4 of Block 4, and Lots 5–7 of Block 4.

The salmon pack figures for the first and poorest year, 1899, were 3,000 cases. The peak year was 1917 with 30,824 cases, and the final year produced 16,227 cases in 1923.[96]

The Simon Leiser and Company agents backed the Skeena River Commercial Cannery in 1898 under the name of Anglo-Alliance Cannery. The plant was located in the central waterfront of Port Essington between Cunningham's Skeena Cannery and the British American plant. BCARS 1/BA/67

Skeena Cannery

Skeena Cannery was located on first part 1.4 acres of Lot 45, Range District, on the south shore of the Skeena River in Port Essington.

1870 — Robert Cunningham, who had served as an assistant to William Duncan on the Metlakatla Indian Reserve under the Church Missionary Society based in England, and later in the employ of the Hudson's Bay Company at Port Simpson, took out a preemption on District Lot 45 (except nine acres that later became the site of the British American Cannery) on the south shore of the Skeena River. He established a general merchandising post to serve the fur trade and the mining industry along the Skeena River and into the Bulkley Valley regions. The area preempted became known as Port Essington.

1883 — Robert Cunningham built a salmon cannery, starting with 40 gillnet fishboats and 225 cannery employees. The cannery was built at the apex of where Lot 45 jutted into the Skeena, giving the plant a command view of the river's estuary. The property consisted of 1.4 acres of land.

1891 — In April, Lot 45, Range 5, Coast District, was Crown Granted to Robert Cunningham.

1891 — One of Port Essington's newspapers, *The Star*, noted that Cunningham was ahead of his time when he installed a freezing plant.

Some of his (Cunningham's) ventures showed keen insight. Such was the installation of a freezing plant in connection with his cannery in 1891. It failed, simply because the eastern markets had not yet been developed.

He was ahead of his time in an enterprise which has since proven one of the most remunerative on the coast.[97]

1899 — On November 10 a major fire at Port Essington (one of many throughout the years), destroyed twenty-three buildings, among them the cannery messhouse of the Skeena plant. Anglo-British Columbia Packing Company's British American Cannery gave Cunningham temporary use of one of their buildings.[98]

1902 — Robert Cunningham sold his Skeena Cannery to British Columbia Packers Association.

1904 — A letter written to Robert Cunningham by R. J. Kerr, Secretary-treasurer of the British Columbia Packers Association in Vancouver, states:

Our solicitors have called to our attention that transfer of the Cunningham Cannery to this company has never been completed. The cannery was taken over three years ago. Also there is a non-completion on your part of 1/3 interest in the water record from Johnson's Creek to Port Essington.[99]

1905 — In April, Robert Cunningham died while in the city of Victoria, B.C. During his years at Port Essington, he had developed the community into a townsite of commercial, industrial, and residential lots, including an Indian Reserve, church properties, and centres for recreation purposes. Some of his business enterprises were large tracts of real estate, sawmills, logging, mining, fur trading, steam boating, and general merchandising. His store comprised an area of 32 × 100 square feet and there were three warehouses.

Built by Robert Cunningham, founder of Port Essington, Skeena Cannery was more
often referred to as Cunningham's Cannery.   BCARS 10779

1906 — In October, the Skeena Cannery and the 1.4
acres of land were transferred through a conveyance in fee
to the British Columbia Packers Association. In 1907 they
became the registered owners of the property.

1921 — British Columbia Fishing and Packing Company became owners of the Skeena Cannery.

1923 — The cannery comprised 22,500 square feet in
area and was 1½ storeys high. It was built on pilings over
the river. Machinery consisted of an Iron Chink, fish knife,
clincher, exhaust box, double seamer, and four cooking
retorts of steel construction steam-heated to maintain ten
pounds pressure.

The plant was powered by steam and gasoline. The
boiler, located within the cannery, was fired by coal and
wood. There was a blacksmith shop, but no can-making
plant, reduction plant, or cold storage plant. The cannery

office was 1,700 square feet and contained a dwelling. Plant
manager was M. K. Dickinson.

Other buildings consisted of housing for the manager
and staff, cottages for employees, Chinese bunkhouse,
Japanese dwelling, and other cannery buildings.

1926 — The cannery closed down.

1934 — British Columbia Packers Limited bought the
Skeena Cannery.

1937 — The plant was closed down around this time.[100]

Some of the tugs used by the plant were the *Chieftain*,
the *Lottie N.*, *Phoenix*, and *Muriel*.

In the early days of the Skeena Cannery operation, Frank
Inrig was one of the plant managers.

The first salmon pack in 1883 produced 7,000 cases. The
poorest year was 1885 with 6,600 cases, and the peak year
was 1924 with 18,001 cases. The final year, 1926, produced
9,476 cases of salmon.[101]

152

Carlisle Cannery

Carlisle Cannery was located on Lot 69, Range 5, Coast District on Telegraph Passage, the southern entrance to the Skeena River.

1894 — John A. Carthew preempted 140 acres of land in February on Lot 69.

1895 — Carlisle Cannery was one of the first to be built outside of the more protected waters of the Skeena River mouth and closer to the newly extended fishing grounds. Where previously the flat-bottomed fishboats had been confined to protected inside waters and had eventually created considerable congestion, the new round-bottom Columbia River type vessels were more seaworthy. They were able to fish the adjacent waters of Chatham Sound and were limited only by weather and rowing distances.

1896 — In February, Carthew paid $140, Certificate of Payment No. 1868, and received the Crown Grant for the property in March. It had been gazetted in May 1894.

1896 — John A. Carthew sold the plant to the Carlisle Packing and Canning Company in March.

1897 — The plant was sold to the Carlisle Canning Company Limited Foreign.

1900 — G. W. Brewster was manager.

1905 — In December, the cannery was sold to Alfred J. Buttimer and George W. Dawson. At that time the buildings were the cannery, China house, bunkhouse, manager's house, blacksmith shop with bellows and flange, charcoal house, two cabins, office, storehouse, messhouse, tar shed, coal bins, Chinese foreman's cabin, and a benzine and lacquer shed. They owned a pile-driver, Rainer No. 1 with steam hammer, two steel blocks for raising the hammer, with 310 feet of 5/8 inch cable and 175 feet of Hercules cable, 36 feet of six ply two inch hose and hawsers.

Plant machinery consisted of one boiler, four retorts, three test kettles, one steel lye kettle with steam coil, twelve sets of new seaming frames, twelve sets of tall cylinders, twenty-four seamers with tall and flat cylinders, one elevator with engine, one Donkey engine with boiler, one power knife (three sizes), one elevator power knife for a filling machine fitted for one pound talls, one steam winch, two pumps, one washer for talls and flats, one washer for halves and flats, three rotary crimpers, and one Letson and Burpee capper for flats.

They also had one Letson and Burpee capper for talls, one Scharke capper and can covers chute, two Jensen filling machines, two Letson and Burpee solder machines (complete with two muriatic acid machines), two square shears and knives, two die presses with two sets each of flat and tall dies, one coal oil system (including fifteen single fire pots, three double fire pots with oil tank air pump and all connections), two hand power fish knives for three sizes, one hand power solder cutter, one chip die for cutting shield, two solder moulds, 520 coolers, thirteen high trucks, eight bathroom trucks, four warehouse trucks, fourteen lacquering trays, two sets of overhead travellers, 700 can trays, one butchering table, four sliming tanks, four washing tanks, one draining table, twelve filling tables, two salting tables, one capping table, one can-mending table, one seaming table, one rinsing tank, and one water reservoir 350 feet north of the cannery.

153

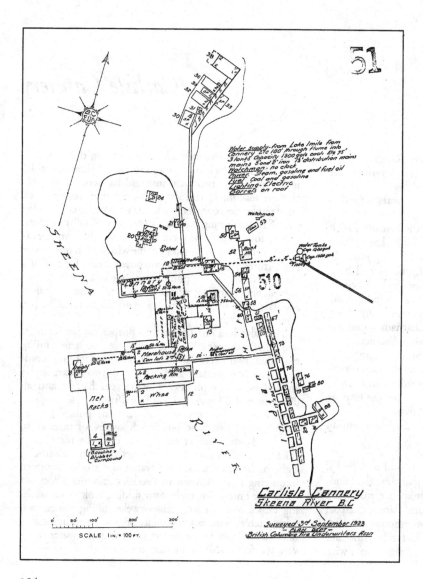

51

Water supply-from Lake 1mile from
Cannery. Ele 180' through Flume into
3 tanks Capacity 1300 gals each. Ele 75'
mains 5 and 2" iron 1½ distribution mains
Watchman- no clock
Power Steam, gasoline and fuel oil
Fuel Coal and gasoline
Lighting-Electric
Barrels on roof

SKEENA

RIVER

Net
Racks

Gasoline +
Blubber
Compound

Carlisle Cannery
Skeena River B.C

Surveyed 3rd September 1923
— PLAN DEPT —
British Columbia Fire Underwriters Assn

SCALE 1 IN. = 100 FT.

They had several scows, among them the *Fannie, Bertha, Annie, May, Flounder, Salmon, Lillie,* and *Shark.* The cannery tug was the *Clive.* Later on they had a steam tug called the *Hong Kong.*[102]

Carlisle Cannery also had its own private telephone line within the complex.

1906 — Carlisle Cannery was sold to the Kildala Packing Company Limited in January for thirty thousand dollars. By this time the plant had a complete Troyer Fox can-making line and produced cans for their own and two other canneries.

1910 — A nine-mile trail was cut through from Carlisle Cannery to Moore's Cove. There was also a boardwalk from Carlisle to the Claxton Cannery.

1923 — The 15,512 square foot cannery building, built over the water on pilings, was two storeys high. Machinery in the plant consisted of a fish knife, two clinchers, two exhaust boxes, two double seamers, and a lacquer machine for a two-line production. Power was supplied by steam, gasoline, and fuel oil. Lighting was provided by a 10 kilowatt, 125 volt dynamo driven by a semi-diesel engine. There were two cooking retorts of wheel construction, steam heated to ten pounds pressure.

Can-manufacturing machinery consisted of three slitting machines, one body-maker machine, one flanger, two double seamers, one tester, two presses, two curling machines, and two compound-applying machines (rubber compound used), three gallon reservoir attached to the machines. Machinery was operated by a twenty-five horsepower Fairbanks-Morse semi-diesel engine, fuel oil fed from a forty gallon tank thirty feet distant and under the wharf. The soldering pot was heated by coal oil. A ten horsepower gasoline engine was used for hauling fish.

An iron clad boilerhouse twenty-eight feet from the cannery was built over pilings. The boiler was fired by coal. There was a 4,800 square foot warehouse, 5,040 square foot packing room, an 868 square foot store and office, and a blacksmith shop. The plant did not have a cold storage or reduction plant.

C. Grafston was manager.

1926 — In September, the Canadian Fishing Company bought the Carlisle Cannery.

1938 — The Haysport Cannery on the Skeena River was dismantled and the machinery brought to the Carlisle Cannery to expand operations there.

1942 — C. Salter was manager of the Carlisle Cannery.

1950 — This was the final year of operation for the Carlisle. The plant machinery was moved to Ocean Dock in Prince Rupert once owned by Nelson Bros. Fisheries and taken over after the Second World War by the Canadian Fishing Company.

1981 — The Canadian Fishing Company was still the registered owner of the Carlisle Cannery site.

The salmon pack for the first year of operation was 7,000 cases in 1895. The poorest year was 1897 with 6,400 cases, and the peak year was 1941 with 72,666 cases. The final year of production was 1950 with 42,560 cases of salmon. In the years of 1928–1932, and again in 1937, the pack statistics were combined with the Haysport Cannery, also owned by the Canadian Fishing Company. There was no canning in 1905.[103]

Carlisle Cannery as it looked when owned by the Canadian Fishing Company.
Until 1949 it was one of three points on the Skeena River from which a 6:00 p.m.
rocket or cannon was discharged to herald the openings and closings for salmon
fishing. The rocket was discharged to such an altitude that it was visible for
miles. WRATHALL

156

The Claxton Cannery was located on Lot 20, Range 5, Coast District, at the mouth of Claxton Creek where it flows into Telegraph Passage along the southern shore to the entrance of the Skeena River.

1888 — With a cash deposit of one dollar an acre Thomas Gamble took out a preemption on Lot 20 for 150 acres.

1890 — In March, with a further payment of $150 Thomas Gamble received the Crown Grant. It had been gazetted in January of 1889.

1891 — On April 1, Thomas Gamble sold the property to Alfred Ingresen.

1891 — Alfred Ingresen sold the land to John Alexander Carthew on April 22.

1891 — The Royal Canadian Packing Company was formed September 19th to establish a fish canning plant at Claxton Creek. Trustees were John Alexander Carthew, Roderick Finlayson, William Dalby, Frederick J. Claxton, and Meyrick Bankes.[104]

1891 — On September 21, John Alexander Carthew sold the property to the Royal Canadian Packing Company Limited.

1892 — A salmon cannery was built at Claxton Creek. It was among the first to be built outside of the more protected waters of the Skeena River mouth and closer to the newly extended fishing grounds. The plant started with twenty fishboats. These were the more seaworthy round-bottom Columbia River type vessels that, unlike flatbottomed fishing boats, were not confined to protected inside waters. Limited only by weather and rowing distances, the new vessels were able to fish the adjacent waters of Chatham Sound.

1893 — John Alexander Carthew was manager of the cannery known as Claxton and often called Royal Canadian. During this time a sawmill was built on the site.

1896 — The Royal Canadian Packing Company Limited applied for and received a Crown Grant on an adjacent 102 acres of land on District Lot 65, bordering Lot 20 on the south side.

1897 — The Royal Canadian Packing Company Limited transferred one-tenth of an acre of Lot 20 and one and three-tenths of an acre of Lot 65 to William Ridley, Bishop of Caledonia, to build a church.

1897 — Claxton Cannery was sold by the Royal Canadian Packing Company to Victoria Packing Company.[105] It was later acquired by Andrew Stewart Robertson.

1900 — Andrew Stewart Robertson sold the cannery and property to John Wallace.

1901 — John Wallace transferred the land and property to Wallace Brothers Packing Company.

1904 — The Royal Canadian Packing Company Limited went into liquidation and the assets were purchased by Peter Wallace of Wallace Brothers Packing Company Limited.

1905 — The Claxton salmon cannery contained one Letson and Burpee power knife, one Letson and Burpee capper, two Letson and Burpee wipers, one Letson and Burpee finger solder machine, one chain solder machine, one weigher, four wooden steam boxes, two old style retorts, and one Pelton wheel.[106]

1906 — A cold storage plant was built. It was 42 feet wide by 165 feet long and two storeys high. Upstairs there was a corridor running across the building into which an elevator, with a capacity of five boxes of fish, was placed. The balance of the floor consisted of two rooms running the length of the building.[107]

1911 — Wallace Brothers Packing Company Limited sold out to Ernest Victor Bodwell on January 30.

1911 — The same day, January 30, Ernest Victor Bodwell sold the plant to Wallace Fisheries Limited.

1911 — It was during this time that the cannery was rebuilt. The plant was run by water power and the cold storage had a forty ton compressor capacity. There were eighty-nine gillnet boats fishing for the company. Peter Wallace was manager.

1911 — On June 29, a letter was written by Peter Wallace to Constable Forsythe at Port Essington reporting a drowning:

Dear Sir—We regret to inform you that an Indian fisherman named Simon Shaw was drowned today at the mouth of the Skeena River off Oceanic Cannery. He was fishing with another Indian named Andrew Lewis (both Kitkatla Indians) Licence No. 2964 Dominion Cannery and 3512 Provincial Cannery (a Rivers Inlet Cannery). When the deceased man fell overboard he was using the pump and was standing on the gunwale in the stern of the boat, with tiller held between his knees and Lewis says he told him to 'look out', as he was in a dangerous position. Andrew Lewis also says that he was using a small hand saw for some purpose at the time of the accident.[108]

1923 — Claxton Cannery was two storeys high, contained 32,288 square feet of space, and had two canning lines. It was built on pilings over the water. Machinery consisted of an Iron Chink, two fish knives, two clinchers, two exhaust boxes, two double seamers, and a lacquer machine. There were five cooking retorts of steel construction, asbestos covered, which operated with ten pounds steam pressure.

Power was supplied by water, fuel oil engine, and gasoline engine. The fuel oil engine was a twenty-five horsepower semi-diesel Fairbanks-Morse, which operated the canning machinery. The gasoline engine was a six horsepower Fairbanks-Morse, which ran the fish haul.

The cold storage plant was a two storey frame building with a metal roof, adjoining the cannery, but not part of it. It was an ammonia system, and the machinery was driven by water power. There was a 5 1/2 kilowatt, 120 volt water power driven dynamo.

The boiler house was thirty-five feet from the cannery, built on pilings and the boiler fueled by coal. A blacksmith shop was located in a separate section of the boiler house. It had a portable forge and a brick furnace.

A 2,464 square foot store and post office was built on pilings close to the cannery complex.

There was no can-manufacturing plant and no fish reduction plant at Claxton Cannery.

Tom Wallace was manager of the cannery.

Claxton Cannery was originally known as Royal Canadian. The plant was the first to be built outside the protected waters of the mouth of the Skeena River and adjacent to the Chatham Sound. BCARS 74565

The Wallace Brothers from Scotland played a large part in the development of the fish processing industry on the British Columbia coast.
BCARS I/BA/C67

1928 — British Columbia Packers Limited purchased the Claxton Cannery.[109] John Clark became manager.

1934 — The cold storage plant at Claxton Cannery burned. The cannery and other buildings were saved by the timely arrival of the Union Steamship vessel *Cardena*, whose personnel helped to put out the fire.

1936 — B.C. Packers Limited installed a re-form line in the cannery. (This machinery rounded out the flattened can bodies that were shipped from the factory in Vancouver).

1944 — The cannery was closed. The net loft was used to store gill and seine nets until 1949.

British Columbia Packers Limited shifted the emphasis of their canning operations on the Skeena River from Claxton to their Sunnyside plant. Sunnyside, located on the Canadian National Railway (formerly the Grand Trunk Pacific) provided rail-shipping access as well as access by steamer.

The salmon pack in the first year of operation at Claxton Cannery was 12,000 cases. The poorest year was 1897 with 6,117 cases. The peak year in 1938 produced 109,083 cases. In the final year, 1944, production was 81,133 cases of salmon.[110]

Wallace Fisheries built a number of packers and seine boats which were known as the "W" boats. In 1925 they built *W No. 7* through *W No. 11*.

Some of the gas tugs that towed the gillnet fleet of sailboats for Claxton were the *Nahmint* and the *Claxton*.

For many years the salmon canneries of the north coast of British Columbia made it a practice to hire university and high school students to work in their plants. This commitment to hiring students enabled many a young person eventually to become a doctor, lawyer, or member of another leading profession. The experiences of one such student worker at Claxton Cannery, Gordon W. Stead, have been recorded in an interview:

I travelled to Claxton Cannery on the *BCP IV*, which was normally used to transport officials to and from Vancouver and to scout for schools of fish. Claxton Cannery, owned then by B.C. Packers, at that time was generally regarded as a high producer—it had three canning lines. John Clarke was manager. I was hired to be assistant storekeeper, but the storekeeper had already hired on an Indian assistant at half the pay.[111]

Stead lived in the attic of the old Mission House, which was being used as a rooming house for white workers. His wages at that time (1929) were seventy-five dollars a month. His duties were varied. He painted licence numbers on the fishboats and repaired and maintained the diesel engines. As the tallyman stationed at the Haysport fishing station for Claxton, across the Skeena, he credited fishermen with the

159

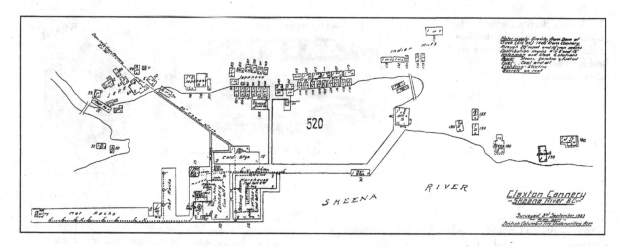

number of each variety of salmon. Often the differences were very subtle, and the price variation was according to type, not size or weight. While at Haysport, Stead was also responsible for the Claxton Cannery mail. It was transported by railway, the train making a whistle stop at Haysport where the mail was picked up.

He worked as the boilerman, replacing the engineer, who got boils. For insurance purposes the engineer had to be present, but Stead did all the work for about two weeks. The boiler was located on pilings over the water, and the coal yard was beside it. Stead's duties consisted of breaking up the bunker coal and stoking the fire with coal during the day and cleaning out the firebox at night. For one week during the peak of canning he worked twenty-two hours a day for three days running, with no overtime pay.

At some point Gordon Stead worked in the cold storage, where steelhead and halibut were frozen and glazed over with hot water.

Stead's last job, on the retorts (cookers), he considered the worst. There was a great deal of condensation in the cookers, so the water was run off into the the ocean to conserve fuel.

The effect of the hot water hitting the cold ocean water was to create a vapour which rose through the floor to be inhaled by the retort workers. Stead considered this very unhealthy.

Stead remembers the Claxton store was as large as a trading post. It was well stocked and did a good business. He remembers that the Haidas were considered the best fishermen and that they lived in a camp on the mountainside. Next were the Japanese, then the Norwegians, and finally the local Indians.

The Chinese contract workers were large men, over six feet tall. They could not speack English and were dominated by their contractor. The Chinese bunkhouse was very self-contained, and the Chinese cannery workers never roamed around the site. There were others who worked as cooks and flunkies. The cooks would prepare anything except fish. Stead ate his meals with the foreman, a handful of operating personnel, the engineer, storekeeper, cold storage manager, and ten to fifteen men, all white. There was no garden or livestock. Supplies could be brought in cheaply from Prince Rupert.

160

Standard Cannery was located on Lot 36, Range 5, Coast District, on Telegraph Passage opposite Kennedy Island.

1889 — In November, Captain John Irving received a Crown Grant of 210 acres of land on Lot 36, Range 5, Coast District.

1889/90—Captain Irving and his associates (R. P. Rithet and J. A. Laidlaw) built a salmon cannery on the site during the winter. The plant was also known as Port Irving Cannery.

Standard Cannery was one of the first to be built out of the more protected waters of the Skeena River mouth and closer to the newly extended fishing grounds. Heretofore, the flat-bottomed fishboats had been confined to protected inside waters, eventually creating considerable congestion. The new round-bottom type vessels, which were more seaworthy, permitted fishermen to work the waters of Chatham Sound, limited only by weather and rowing distances. Thus, the entire salmon fishing industry began to move out of the early confinement, into open waters, and eventually toward the more consolidated urban transportation centres.

Captain John Irving was the son of William Irving, who had been in the British mercantile marine and was an enterprising steamboat owner on the British Columbia coast. John inherited his father's businesses. He went on to establish the Canadian Pacific Navigation Company, later to be purchased by the Canadian Pacific Railway.[112]

1892 — Captain John Irving sold the Standard Cannery to the Victoria Canning Company of British Columbia Limited.

1896 — Frank Inrig was manager of the cannery.

1902 — Standard Cannery was purchased by British Columbia Packers Association.

1903 — Standard Cannery was closed. It was then used as a fish camp for Balmoral Cannery and later for Claxton Cannery.[113]

1921 — Standard Cannery became the property of British Columbia Fishing and Packing Company.

1934 — British Columbia Packers Limited took ownership of the property.

Standard Cannery had a can-making plant and made their own wooden boxes for shipping cases.

A memo in the Henry Doyle papers lists some of the plant inventory for 1902. On hand was:

876 boxes of 12 × 20 inch tinplate for making 5160 cases of ½ pound flat cans.
726 boxes of 14 × 20 inch tinplate for making 6649 cases of one-pound tall cans.
Solder—15,311 pounds.
Salt—6,330 pounds.
Charcoal—1,872 barrels.
Fuel—32 tons of coal and 118 cords of wood.
Caustic soda—5 or 6 drums.
Acid—10 cartons.
Lacquer—158 gallons.
Benzine—76 cases.
Box nails—15 kegs.[114]

The salmon pack for the first year of operation in 1890 was 10,600 cases. The poorest year was 1897 with 4,600 cases, and the peak year was 1900 with 12,000 cases. The final year of operation in 1902 produced 11,977 cases of salmon.[115]

Standard Cannery, the most southern of the Skeena canneries, as it looked in 1903, the year it closed down.   PAC/PA 118172

162

Oceanic Cannery

Oceanic Cannery was located on Lot 10, Range 5, Coast District, on the south side of Smith Island at the entrance to the mouth of the Skeena River.

1884 — In December, a Crown Grant was issued to Henry Edward Croasdaile in fee of Lot 10, Range 5, Coast District containing 161 acres of land.

1885 — In January, Henry Edward Croasdaile sold the property to John Herbert Turner.

1892 — A mortgage indenture was made whereby J. H. Turner and Henry Coppinger Beeton granted and conveyed Lot 10, Range 5, Coast District to Charles Leggatt and his heirs to the use of the said J. H. Turner and Robert Arthur Lawrence Kirk in fee as joint tenants.

1892 — Henry Coppinger Beeton held a mortgage against the property until April of 1902.

1900 — The Bank of British Columbia held a mortgage against the land until December 1901.

1901 — John Herbert Turner and Robert Arthur Lawrence Kirk sold the site to Charles Fox Todd and Albert Edward Todd.

1902 — The property was sold in December to the British Columbia Canning Company Limited.

1903 — Oceanic Cannery was built to replace the British Columbia Canning Company's Aberdeen Cannery further up the Skeena River, which had burned the previous year. Moving out of the river mouth was part of a general trend in the industry to avoid overcrowding of plants, a high concentration of fishing vessels in the immediate estuary, and to take advantage of an expanded fishery due to the range of larger, more seaworthy fishing craft.

1910 — A. W. Carter was manager of the cannery.

1911 — There were many tragedies among the vessels of the fishing fleet. A letter expressing concern over such an incident was written June 26th by Oceanic Cannery manager A. W. Carter to Alexander Forsythe, Constable at Port Essington. It states:

The Captain of the tug, "Escort No. 2" reported to me yesterday that he had run down one of our fishing boats on Friday night and the occupants were evidently drowned. The boat was taken away on Friday evening by a man named Charlie Lawrence with the intention of going to Essington for his partner. Whether he went and got him or whether he went outside alone we cannot say. But I am inclined to think he went alone. He fished at Balmoral last season. Could you find out anything about him so that his friends could be notified. He left no trace on anything here.[116]

1923 — Oceanic Cannery was 20,240 square feet in area. It was built on pilings and its height was 3 1/2 storeys. It had two canning lines, and machinery consisted of an Iron Chink, two fish knives, three weighing machines, three salt machines, slimer, three clinchers, three exhaust boxes, and a lacquer machine. There were four cooking retorts of steel construction. The plant was powered by steam, water, and gasoline. One five horsepower Fairbanks-Morse operated the fish haul and a six horsepower Fairbanks-Morse operated the Iron Chink. The labeling machine was water power operated. There had once been a cold storage plant but no reduction plant or can-manufacturing plant. The boiler house was located thirty feet from the cannery, and the boiler was fueled by wood. There was a blacksmith shop.

Oceanic Cannery was built on Smith Island in the mouth of the Skeena River to replace Aberdeen (Windsor) Cannery, which had burned down. Thirty-two years later Oceanic was also razed by fire.   PRINCE RUPERT DAILY NEWS

The Oceanic Cannery label under the British ▶
Columbia Canning Company Limited.

The store and office was 1,200 square feet. Other buildings were a messhouse, Chinese bunkhouse, Japanese housing, a general bunkhouse, salt shed, housing for management, a large number of Indian dwellings, and a church.

1924 — In April the British Columbia Fishing and Packing Company Limited took over ownership of the Oceanic plant.

1928 — The British Columbia Fishing and Packing Company became part of the amalgamation that formed British Columbia Packers Limited.

1929 — The cannery was closed. But the plant operated as a fish camp for Claxton until the end of 1931.

1932 — Robert Gosse owned the plant.

1933 — The plant was sold to Ocean Salmon Canneries Limited in June.

1935 — The plant was destroyed by fire.

1936 — The Oceanic Cannery property was purchased by the Canadian Fishing Company. They built a fish camp there and operated it until 1950.

Two of the tugs for towing gillnet vessels used by Oceanic were the *Eva* and the *Bamberton*. The *Bamberton* was skippered by one of the first native Indian skippers on the coast.

The first year's salmon pack in 1903 was 13,941 cases. The poorest year was 1913 with 10,790 cases, and the peak year was 1934 with 39,788 cases. The final year of canning in 1935 produced 12,493 cases. The plant did not can in the years of 1923, 1924, 1929–1932.[117]

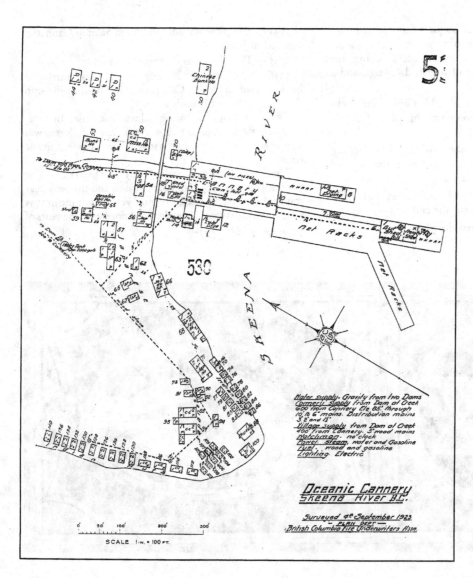

Water supply- Gravity from two Dams
Cannery supply from Dam at Creek
600' from Cannery Ele. 85', through
10' to 6' mains. Distribution mains
3,2 and 15'.
Village supply from Dam at Creek
400' from Cannery. 3' wood mains
Watchman - no clock
Power- steam, water and Gasoline
Fuel, wood and gasoline
Lighting. Electric

Oceanic Cannery
Skeena River B.C.

Surveyed 4th September 1923
PLAN by
British Columbia Fire Underwriters Assn.

0'   50'   100'   200'   300'

SCALE 1 IN. = 100 FT.

With their barrel-shaped ▶
roofs, the buildings of
Humpback Bay Cannery,
Porcher Island, were unique
in their design and structure.

WRATHALL 1933

Humpback Bay Cannery

Humpback Bay Cannery was located on Lot B of District Lot 7313, Range 5, Coast District, Plan 1593, an 18.36 acre block of land in Humpback Bay on the north end of Porcher Island adjacent to the mouth of the Skeena River.

1928 — Chatham Sound Fishing and Packing Company built Humpback Bay Cannery under the direction of F.H. Cunningham, who had been Chief Inspector of Fisheries in British Columbia from 1911 to 1921. Cunningham either owned, or had an interest in, the company.[118]

The land at that time was owned by the Crown.

1931 — The land, forty-four acres, was Crown Granted to Elbert Donaldson Hogan and Lewis Wiley Hogan.

1933 — The cannery no longer operated as a canning plant.

1934 — The Canadian Fishing Company operated the cannery as a maintenance, boat, and net station.

1936 — James Skinner owned the property on which the cannery was built: 18.36 acres.

1943 — The Canadian Fishing Company purchased the property from James Skinner.

Before coming under jurisdiction of the Oceanside Plant managers in Prince Rupert, the plant was managed by Cunningham, Hogan, and Terry Olsen.

The year's salmon pack in 1929 was 18,790 cases. In the final year, 1932, the pack was 24,531 cases. The 1930–31 packs were totaled with that of the Haysport Cannery, also owned by the Canadian Fishing Company Limited.[119]

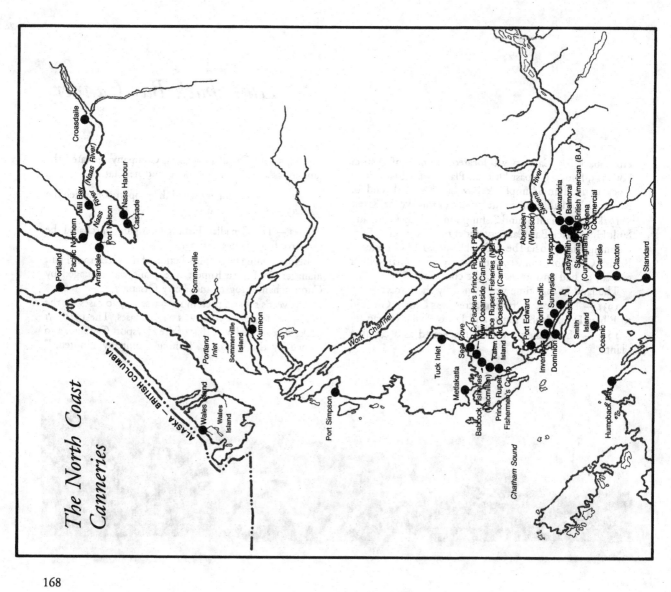

The North Coast Canneries

Croasdaile
Mill Bay (Naas River)
Nass River
Nass Harbour
Nass River
Cascade
Port Nelson
Pacific Northern
Arrandale
Portland
Sommerville
Sommerville Island
Kumeon
Portland Inlet
Wales Sound
Wales Island
ALASKA – BRITISH COLUMBIA
Work Channel
Tuck Inlet
Metlakatla
Port Simpson
Babcock Fisheries (Macmillan)
Prince Rupert Fishermen's Co-op
Seal Cove
Packers Prince Rupert Plant
New Oceanside (CanFisCo)
Kaien Island
Prince Rupert Fisheries (NPF)
Old Oceanside (CanFisCo)
Port Edward
Inverness
North Pacific
Dominion
Sunnyside
Smith Island
Oceanic
Aberdeen (Windsor)
Hayspad
Ladysmith
Skeena (Cunningham), Skeena
North Pacific
Alexandria
Balmoral
British American (B.A.)
Commercial
Carlisle
Claxton
Standard
Skeena River
Chatham Sound
Humpback Bay

168

Endnotes

1 Canada Sessional Papers, *Fisheries Commissioner's Report*, 1903.

2 Catalogue No. 9, Edward Lipsett Limited, page 425.

3 Interview with Bill Ross, former net-man and manager of North Pacific Cannery on the Skeena River.

4 Captain Don Peck, "Skeena River Memories Before Power Gillnetters," *Daily Colonist*, July 1, 1972.

5 Duncan Stacey, *Sockeye and Tinplate. Technological Change in the Fraser River Canning Industry 1871–1912*, British Columbia Provincial Museum, Victoria, B.C., 1982.

6 Catalogue Number 9, Edward Lipsett Limited.

7 *Ibid.*

8 *Ibid.*, Page 419

9 *Ibid.*, page 425

10 Alfred Carmichael, "An Account of a Season's Work at a Salmon Cannery; Windsor; Aberdeen; Skeena," 1891, Provincial Archives of British Columbia manuscript.

11 The Henry Doyle Notes, Box 4, Special Collections Library, University of British Columbia.

12 As told to retired cannery lineman Doug Browne of Cassidy, B.C. by an elderly Chinese cannery worker.

13 Personal interview with Mrs. L. J. North.

14 Willam M. Ross, "Operating Canneries on the Nass River 1881–1945," University of British Columbia, Vancouver, B.C.

15 1917 Doyle Diaries — Box 4, Special Collections Library, University of British Columbia.

16 William M. Ross, "Operating Canneries on the Nass River 1881–1945."

17 Chronological Record of Henry Doyle's Connections with the British Columbia Salmon Fisheries, Appendix #1, Special Collections Library, University of British Columbia.

18 Cicely Lyons, *Salmon: Our Heritage*, Mitchell Press, Vancouver, B.C. 1969, page 167.

19 *Ibid.*, page 166.

20 William M. Ross, "Operating Canneries on the Nass River 1881–1945."

21 1908 Booklet, Doyle Papers — Box 4, Special Collections Library, University of British Columbia.

22 *Ibid.*

23 *Ibid.*

24 *Ibid.*

25 *Ibid.*

26 *Ibid.*

27 *Ibid.*

28 Public Archives of Canada, List of Fishing Stations and Rights Allotted to Indians by the Indian Reserve Commission, Extract RG 10, Vol. 3908, File 107297—1.

29 William M. Ross, "Operating Canneries on the Nass River 1881–1945."

30 *Victoria Daily Colonist*, March 10, 1894.

31 William M. Ross, "Operating Canneries on the Nass River 1881–1945."

32 *Ibid.*

33 *Ibid.*

34 Doyle Papers — Box 4, University of British Columbia Special Collections.

35 William M. Ross, "Operating Canneries on the Nass River 1881–1945."

36 *Ibid.*

37 1908 Booklet, Doyle Papers — Box 4, Special Collections Library, University of British Columbia.

38 *Ibid.*

39 William M. Ross, "Operating Canneries on the Nass River 1881–1945."

40 *Ibid.*

41 *Ibid.*

42 Doyle Papers — Box 4, University of British Columbia Special Collections.

43 William M. Ross, "Operating Canneries on the Nass River 1881–1945."

44 Information courtesy of Robert Strand.

45 William M. Ross, "Operating Canneries Skeena River 1877–1966.

46 *Prince Rupert Daily News*, January 27, 1912.

47 William M. Ross, "Operating Canneries Skeena River 1877–1966."

48 Cicely Lyons, *Salmon: Our Heritage*, Pages 387–389.

49 William M. Ross, "Operating Canneries Skeena River 1877—1966."

50 *Ibid.*

51 The Canadian Fishing Company statistics — courtesy Tom Brennan and Gail Bergen.

169

[52] British Columbia Packers Limited Statistics — courtesy of Conrad Ganzenberg.

[53] British Columbia Packers Statistics — courtesy Laurie Nolan.

[54] Courtesy of Gordon Lindquist of McMillan Fisheries.

[55] Courtesy of Joe Ward.

[56] William M. Ross, "Operating Canneries Skeena River 1877–1966."

[57] *The Canadian Fishing Company Statistics* — courtesy of Gail Bergen and Tom Brennan

[58] Prince Rupert Fishermen's Co-operative Association — courtesy of Robert Strand.

[59] Information courtesy of Ken Harding, General Manager of the Prince Rupert Fishermen's Co-operative Association.

[60] Provincial Archives of British Columbia MS — 1/BA/M22. Notes on the Names and History of the Plants of British Columbia Packers Limited, 1939.

[61] William M. Ross, "Operating Canneries Skeena River 1877–1966."

[62] British Columbia Packers Limited Statistics, courtesy of Conrad Ganzenberg.

[63] Information courtesy of Conrad Ganzenberg.

[64] Henry Doyle Diaries — Box 4, Special Collections Library, University of British Columbia .

[65] Keith Philippson, personal notes, Prince Rupert, B.C., 1976.

[66] Howard Melo notes, Prince Rupert, B.C., 1978.

[67] Keith Philippson notes.

[68] William M. Ross, "Operating Canneries Skeena River 1877–1966."

[69] *British Columbia Gazette*, January 3, 1889, page 11.

[70] Keith Philippson notes.

[71] William M. Ross, "Operating Canneries Skeena River 1877–1966."

[72] The Canadian Fishing Company Statistics, courtesy Gail Bergen and Tom Brennan.

[73] Keith Philippson notes.

[74] Cicely Lyons, *Salmon: Our Heritage*, page 260.

[75] William M. Ross, "Operating Canneries Skeena River 1877–1966."

[76] *Ibid.*

[77] B.C. Packers statistics courtesy of Conrad Ganzenberg.

[78] Doyle Collection, Box 4, General Notes — northern canneries, Special Collections Library, University of British Columbia.

[79] Keith Philippson notes.

[80] Doyle Records, General Notes, 1915–1922, Box 4, Special Collections, University of British Columbia.

[81] *Ibid.*

[82] *Ibid.*

[83] William M. Ross, "Operating Canneries Skeena River 1877–1966."

[84] *Victoria Colonist*, June 13, 1895.

[85] William M. Ross, "Operating Canneries Skeena River 1877–1966."

[86] *Ibid.*

[87] Henry Doyle Papers — Letters Incoming, Folder 1-3, Special Collections Library, University of British Columbia.

[88] *Daily Colonist*, July 1, 1972.

[89] William M. Ross, "Operating Canneries Skeena River 1877–1966."

[90] *Ibid.*

[91] *Ibid.*

[92] *Ibid.* and *Henderson's British Columbia Gazetteer and Directory 1900–01*, pp. 159–160.

[93] William M. Ross, "Operating Canneries Skeena River 1877–1966."

[94] *Ibid.*

[95] Doyle Notes, Box 4, Special Collections, University of British Columbia.

[96] William M. Ross, "Operating Canneries Skeena River 1877–1966."

[97] *The Star*, Port Essington, July 18, 1908.

[98] Keith Philippson, notes.

[99] *Ibid.*

[100] Cicely Lyons, *Salmon: Our Heritage*, page 679.

[101] William M. Ross, "Operating Canneries Skeena River 1877–1966."

[102] Doyle Papers — Box 4, Special Collections, University of British Columbia, Pages 206–209.

[103] William M. Ross, "Operating Canneries Skeena River 1877–1966."

[104] *B.C. Gazette*, September 24, 1891.

[105] Cicely Lyons, *Salmon: Our Heritage*, page 228.

[106] Henry Doyle Papers, Box 4, Special Collections Library, University of British Columbia.

[107] *Ibid.*

[108] Keith Philippson notes.

[109] Cicely Lyons, *Salmon: Our Heritage*, page 201.

[110] William M. Ross, "Operating Canneries Skeena River 1877–1966."

[111] Interview with Gordon W. Stead, Vancouver, B.C., by Dr. Dianne Newell, Department of History, UBC.

[112] John T. Walbran, *British Columbia Coast Names 1592–1906*, published for Vancouver Public Library by J. J. Douglas, page 290.

[113] Cicely Lyons, *Salmon: Our Heritage*, page 679.

[114] Henry Doyle Papers, Box 4, memo, Special Collections Library, University of British Columbia.

[115] William M. Ross, "Operating Canneries Skeena River 1877–1966."

[116] Keith Philippson notes.

[117] William M. Ross, "Operating Canneries Skeena River 1877–1966."

[118] Cicely Lyons, *Salmon: Our Heritage*, page 523.

[119] William M. Ross, "Operating Canneries Skeena River 1877–1966."

Andrews, Ralph W. and Larsen, A. K. *Fish and Ships*. Superior Publishing Company, Seattle, Washington. 1959.

Blyth, Alex. Interviews. Port Edward, B.C. 1973–1989

British Columbia Gazette.

British Columbia Fire Underwriters Association, Planning Department. "Plans of Salmon Canneries in British Columbia with Inspection Reports on Each." August 1924.

British Columbia Packers Limited Statistics.

Browne, Douglas. Interviews. Cassidy, B.C. 1981.

Canada Sessional Papers, 1891. Annual Report: "Schedule of Salmon Canneries in Existence in British Columbia in the Season of 1890." Department of Fisheries Appendix F, 180-1, Ottawa.

Canada Sessional Papers, 1903. Fisheries Commissioner's Report.

The Canadian Fishing Company Statistics.

Carmichael, Alfred. "An Account of a Season's Work at a Salmon Cannery." MS in Provincial Archives, Victoria, B.C. 1891.

Chettleburgh, Peter. "Overabundance was an Embarrassment." *Western Fisheries*, Vancouver, B.C. September 1979.

Cobb, John N. *The Canning of Fishery Products*. Miller Freeman, Publisher, Seattle, WA. 1919.

Department of Environment. "Salmon Trolling in British Columbia." Government of Canada, Ottawa.

Doyle, Henry. Chronological Record of Henry Doyle with the British Columbia Salmon Fisheries, Appendix #1. Special Collections, University of British Columbia, Vancouver, B.C.

_____. 1908 Booklet. Special Collections Library, University of British Columbia, Vancouver, B.C.

_____. Letters Incoming, Folder 1-3. Special Collections Library, University of British Columbia, Vancouver, B.C.

_____. Uncatalogued Papers. Special Collections, University of British Columbia.

Evans, Hubert. "Day of the Hand Troller." *Raincoast Chronicles First Five — Collector's Edition: Stories and History of the B.C. Coast*. Harbour Publishing, Madeira Park, B.C.

Fisheries and Oceans. Fact Sheets— "The Life Cycle of Pacific Salmon." Information Branch, Vancouver, B.C.

Forrester, Joseph E., and Forrester, Anne D. *Fishing: British Columbia's Commercial Fishing History*. Hancock House Publishers, Ltd., Saanichton, B.C. 1975.

Gosnell, R.E. "The Fisheries." *The Yearbook of British Columbia and Manual of Information*. Victoria, B.C. 1911.

Henderson's British Columbia Gazeteer and Directory 1900–1901. Provincial Archives of British Columbia, Victoria, B.C.

Hill, A.V. *Tides of Change*. Published by Prince Rupert Fishermen's Co-operative Association. Evergreen Press, Vancouver, B.C.

Land Registry Office. Prince Rupert, B.C.

Lawrence, J.C. "An Historical Account of the Early Salmon Industry in British Columbia, 1870–1900." Unpublished graduating essay, Department of History, University of British Columbia, Vancouver, B.C. 1951.

Edward Lipsett Ltd. Catalogue No. 9. Vancouver, B.C.

Lyons, Cicely. *Salmon: Our Heritage*. Mitchell Press, Vancouver, B.C. 1969.

McKervill, Hugh. *The Salmon People: The Story of Canada's West Coast Salmon Fishing Industry of British Columbia*. Gray's Publishing, Vancouver, B.C. 1967.

Melo, Howard. Notes. Prince Rupert, B.C. 1978.

Nelson Bros. Fisheries Ltd. "The Story of the Canned Salmon Industry of British Columbia." Nelson Bros. Fisheries Ltd. Occupational Series No.1-C-1.

North, Mrs. L. J. Interview. Prince Rupert, B.C. 1980.

Peck, Captain Don. "Skeena River Memories Before Power Gillnetters," *The Daily Colonist*, (Victoria, B.C.), Saturday, July 1, 1972.

Philips, Richard H. "The History of Western Seining," *National Fisherman*, (Seattle, Washington) Vol. 52, No. 5, September, 1971.

Philippson, Keith. Interviews and personal notes. Prince Rupert, B.C. 1976.

Prince Rupert Daily News

Provincial Archives of British Columbia. MS-1/BA/M22 "Notes on the Names and History of the Plants of British Columbia Packers Ltd." 1939.

Public Archives of Canada. List of Fishing Stations and Rights Allotted to Indians by the Indian Reserve Commission, Extract RG 10, Vol. 3908, File 107297-1.

Ross, William M. "Operating Canneries Skeena River 1877–1966." University of British Columbia, Vancouver, B.C.

——. "Number of Operating Canneries on the Nass and Skeena Rivers. 1900–1914." Unpublished graduating essay, University of British Columbia, Vancouver, B.C.

——. "Operating Canneries on the Nass River 1881–1945." University of British Columbia, Vancouver, B.C.

——. "Salmon Canning Distribution on the Nass and Skeena Rivers of British Columbia 1877–1926." University of British Columbia, Vancouver, B.C.

——. Interviews. Richmond, B.C. and Prince Rupert, B.C. 1978–1984.

Sharcott, Margaret. "Century of Fishing." *The Daily Colonist* (Victoria, B.C.). Saturday, July 1, 1967.

Stacey, Duncan. *Sockeye and Tinplate: Technological Change in the Fraser River Canning Industry 1871–1912*. British Columbia Provincial Museum, Victoria, B.C. 1982.

The Star. Port Essington, British Columbia.

Victoria Daily Colonist. Victoria, B.C.

Walbran, John T., *British Columbia Coast Names 1592–1906*. Published for Vancouver Public Library by J.J. Douglas. 1977.

Photo Credits

British Columbia Archives Record Service (BCARS)
Public Archives Canada (PAC)
Prince Rupert Regional Archives, Barbara Sheppard
Special Collections Library,
  University of British Columbia
Ian Bell-Irving, Vancouver, B.C.
Phylis Bowman, Port Edward, B.C.
Ken Dopson, Prince Rupert, B.C.
Roy Honda
Mrs. L. J. North, Prince Rupert, B.C.
Al Price
Prince Rupert Daily News
Bill and Honey Ross, Steveston, B.C.

Acknowledgements

My interest in the history of the salmon fishing and canning industry ran concurrent with my husband's life and work in the industry. Living the cannery life, attuned to the sea, the fishermen, the shoreworkers, made me aware of the multitude of stories to be told, to be written.

This avid interest in the history and the stories of Canada's dynamic west coast fishery led me through the reading and research of many writings, some long forgotten. But the essence of the texts remained with me to provide a depth of understanding which greatly assisted in the final selection of materials for this writing.

The same was true of the countless conversations and dialogues I overheard or witnessed among the participants in the industry. Few realized that "someone" was gullibly eavesdropping, forever asking pertinent questions, savouring their stories, cherishing every descriptive word be it wild or rational. All of this I stored in a file of remembrances against the day when some of it would be recorded. My appreciation goes out to these inadvertent sources, whoever you were/are.

Special thanks to the following people, most of them friends, who generously provided information, timely advice, or help—Jake Nelson, Don Mcleod, William Babcock, Norman Gobles, Brian Hayward, Duncan Stacey, Bill and Honey Ross, Mrs. L. J. North, Doug Browne, William M. Ross, Gordon Lindquist, Conrad Ganzenberg, Laurie Nolan, Tom Brennan, Gail Bergen, Joe Ward, Robert Strand, Ken Harding, Gene Simpson, Keith Philippson, Howard Melo, Herb Glover, Dr. Dianne Newell, Mel Hubbell, John Atchison, Lloyd and Dorothy Booth, Jimmy Donaldson, George and Josie Newton, Bill Lawson, Dr. and Mrs. Arthur Gallagher, Harry Robins, Allan Hale, Bill Hale, Fred Edgar, Harvey Atchison, Gordon and Effie Ronson, Henry Reid, Ken Campbell, Cliff Armstrong, Ron Denman, George McGregor, Ed Bolton, John McGregor, Bill Rothwell, Terry Olsen, Robert Stewart, Teo Okabe, Ole Olafson, Ted Moore, Selina Starr, Mike Postak, Les and Chris Yates, and many others.

Thanks also to the Land Registry Office of Prince Rupert, British Columbia Packers Limited, McMillan Fisheries, and the Prince Rupert Fishermen's Co-operative Association.

A special thanks to my husband, Alex, who shared with me his vast and timely knowledge of the fishing industry—thereby providing the continuity so essential to the recording of this history.

Because the history of the fishing industry encompasses the entire British Columbia coast, and the lives of many hundreds of thousands of people, there is still much to be documented. I hope others will be stirred to do more research, to seek out the veterans of all the coastal fisheries and to record their memories before they fade into oblivion.

Index

176

178

Printed in the United States
By Bookmasters